GIVING WOMEN

A V

G000066146

A collaboration of real-life stories

from survivors of abuse

Compiled by Donna Anne Pace

Foreword by Dr. Miriam Dalli MEP

To Judith and the team at The Rising Sun charity Love and best wishes to you all, from Ann Marina

Dedicated to women around the world

who have overcome the unimaginable.

Let us all take a moment to think about all

the women who are now Angels.

This book gives a voice to domestic violence
survivors,

and to women around the world

whose voices will never sadly

be heard again.

Marina Longster

TABLE OF CONTENTS

BOOK REVIEWS

Giving Woman a Voice is a collaboration of true stories by women who have survived grievous emotional and physical abuse. I could not put this book down. Few betrayals are as gut-wrenching as being abused by the man these women should have been able to trust with their lives.

Each story was an important history. Each story reminds the reader that nothing in human civilization can be wholly enjoyed and celebrated so long as women and children suffer domestic abuse.

This book is filled with personal stories of threats, beatings, and sexual abuse, but is layered with personal triumphs, as so many of the victims turn sorrow into joy and we learn that innocent people can win, and can change their lives, and can help others.

I wish this book could be required reading for all adults on this earth, and if such were to happen, I believe that we could make great strides in eliminating the violence against women and children, and that is a worthy goal for our civilization to reach.

You say you want to help? Help by reading this book and passing the word, and never turning away from a situation where you know there is a victim who needs your help'!

Jean Sasson

Author

The Princess Sultana Series and other books about brave women who overcame violent abuse

'An insight into the often silent horror of coercive behaviour, told by women who have been there, endured that, and come out the other side. This book shines a light into a world that, until recently, was often misunderstood and ignored. An important read'.

Liz Cooke

Novelist

Foreword

Dr. Miriam Dalli MEP

The phrase 'sharing is caring' is severely overused. However, this anthology project is a clear example of how sharing experiences is indeed an act of caring. Although the modern world has seen advances in more ways than we can describe in writing, some experiences are still worth sharing because the progress in their regard has been very limited.

Domestic abuse is one of these aspects. It is incomprehensible that women, men, and children around the world are still falling prey within the four walls that they call home; the place where they should be able to feel safe and actually be safe.

The very fact that domestic abuse happens in the comfort of one's home means that unless we find victims who are brave enough to communicate their plight, we will never fully understand the ways in which we can reach out and help. Perhaps we will realize that help is needed when it is too late; when victims have already endured endless psychological or physical harm, when they lose all sense of ambition and aspiration in life, or when their very life is taken away from them.

Unless we find people willing to listen, document, and act on these shared experiences, we will never understand how important it is to take a stand. One shared experience can be enough to encourage another victim to share their experience. One shared experience can be enough to revise the way in which we, policymakers, look at domestic violence, discuss ways of addressing and implementing measures that stop this international epidemic.

I am a firm believer in the importance of education. Let us, as adults, share what we know about domestic violence with school-aged children so that they learn at a very tender age that certain behaviour is completely unacceptable. I believe this will help in preventing future adults from eventually becoming both victims and perpetrators.

I also firmly believe that national authorities should never cease to find ways of being more vigilant, more sensitive, more efficient in handling cases of domestic violence. Once an experience is shared with the police, once it is heard in the law courts, once a child speaks up at school, once a person confides in their work colleague, once an abused teenager talks to a care worker, once a doctor comes across a suspected case of abuse, there needs to be impeccable safety, clarity, and optimization in the way that shared experience is handled.

This is a major challenge that we face. I commend this project for helping us reach that aim and I reiterate my commitment to lending an ear to these shared experiences and making sure that they were not shared in vain.

Dr. Miriam Dalli, MEP

February 2020

Malta

INTRODUCTION

Hello and welcome to Giving Women A Voice. My name is Donna Anne Pace and I'm a survivor of domestic violence. I am fully aware of the repercussions of speaking up since breaking my silence in March 2018 with the publication of my first book *The Reinvention of Me - a journey of self-discovery in a disenchanted world.* This was a prominent time in my life which became embroiled in emotional and physical pain that I was not prepared for. So why did I choose to break my silence, you may be asking yourself right now?

I made the decision to share my story and began a campaign to start speaking up publicly through the press and social media in the UK, USA, and Malta, about the horrors of abuse that I have either witnessed or endured since childhood into adulthood. I decided that my newfound confidence and self-worth was going to become the platform upon which I would help other survivors of abuse. I do not believe that any woman, man, or child should ever suffer such despicable emotional and/or physical trauma at the hands of another human being.

Giving Women A Voice features real-life, survivor-led courageous stories from women living in the UK, USA, and Malta, who have all endured different forms of abuse at the hands of an intimate or non-intimate partner. Ten tenacious co-authors who have made the very brave decision to relive the horrors of their past in order to find a new path to healing and embrace a brighter future.

This book that you hold in the palm of your hand right now has been 22 months in the making. Throughout this timeline, there have been many occasions when I have just felt like giving up. Not because of a lack of self-belief or inability to complete a project. I felt like giving up because of succumbing to physical health issues; on-going family estrangement (from some members of my family); a degree of on-going psychological abuse from my abuser and one of my siblings, and also hostility from some people living in the local community who seek to character assassinate me amongst their social network.

I grew up in London into a mixed-race family – English & Maltese, and my upbringing was predominantly Maltese; quite strict and somewhat biased. At the age of 23 I moved to Malta, got married at 24 and settled into my new life. Yet little did I know that from the moment I said my wedding vows that I was embarking upon becoming my husband's possession. The abuse that I endured was subtle and sometimes I didn't even know what was happening. When I did understand I tried to protect my children from it but later I learnt that children *hear* - you may protect them from seeing things, but they still know.

11

I made the decision a few years ago to separate and a year later filed for divorce. I could not afford to hire a Solicitor, so I taught myself how to complete the necessary documents to submit to the Family Court, and I also wrote my own report. I was on an emotional rollercoaster as one of my parent's, my siblings, some of my extended family members, along with some mutual friends, backed away from me and decided to ostracise me. But my determination and hard work eventually paid off when I received my *decree absolute* in the post declaring that my marriage was finally dissolved on the grounds of my husband's unreasonable behavior.

In 2017 I decided to put my thoughts and emotions into words and found it very cathartic. From one word, one sentence, one paragraph, I started to formulate a book, a book that encompassed a myriad of life experiences – from the tragic loss of one of my beloved children to the horrors I faced during childhood when my mum use to lock me up in the bathroom to make me watch her self-harm. A book that was filled with raw emotions, behaviours, traumas, and also an air of positivity. A book that would finally set me free!

In 2018 I started receiving malicious communications from my twin sister who did not take kindly to me publishing my first book, and the subject matter I wrote about. The communications I received via Facebook were so offensive that I reported the content to the Police.

Here are those comments:

'Donna you're a joke and your book is a joke. How dare you disrespect Dad, just remember, what goes around comes around'.

'Donna, you are a selfish b**** and you are going to end up a lonely old woman'

'You're a poor excuse of a mum and don't deserve your children'.

These are just some of the spiteful, bitter comments that I received from my twin in 2018. It's also not uncommon for me to receive random malicious comments from unknown women who use the same narrative as my twin. You see, here's the thing. When people have some degree of control over your life – telling you how you should live, what you should wear, who you should date, and constantly berate you about your looks or personality – until that time when you find the courage to speak up. That's when the abuser realises they are losing their control over you, so they resort to becoming a keyboard warrior. Hiding behind the confines of their device, spurting hate and lies in order to make themselves feel better about who they are. Because, truth be told, abusers find it much easier to character assassinate someone else instead of actually taking a good hard look within themselves to accept who they truly are. Denial and ignorance are their coping mechanisms.

Finding the courage to speak up about your life experiences will not always resonate or be understood by some people, albeit family, friends, co-workers, etc. Your life is YOUR life – it's as simple as that! The decisions or choices you made in the past, present, and which you will go on to make in the future, will be done consciously, and subconsciously, with one goal in mind – to be happy. After all, isn't that what most human beings are striving for? Go with your gut instinct when faced with a challenge, for that instinct could be your saving grace, it could save your life or the life of another human being.

I am very passionate about helping other women find their inner strength and courage to find their voice! To realise their own self-worth and capabilities – traits of their personalities that have been chipped away over time by their abuser. You are all capable of achieving such amazing things in your life. Never stop believing in yourself, your goals, your dreams. Create a supportive network and reach out for help when you need it. Never feel ashamed for asking for help, for this will be one of the bravest things you will ever do!

As you will go on to read throughout this amazingly powerful book, every empowering co-author has one common connection – irrespective of age, ethnicity, location, or religious beliefs – they are SURVIVORS! It is so very sad that even in the 21st Century, millions of people worldwide are enduring daily torture, albeit psychologically and/or physically.

What is Domestic Abuse?

Domestic abuse is more than physical violence. It can also include, but is not limited to:

- coercive control and 'gaslighting'
- economic abuse
- online abuse
- verbal abuse
- emotional abuse
- sexual abuse

Statistics on Domestic Violence

(Credit: refuge.org.uk)

Almost one in three women aged 16-59 will experience domestic abuse in her lifetime
Office for National Statistics (2019) Domestic abuse in England and Wales overview: November 2019

Two women a week are killed by a current or former partner in England and Wales alone
Office for National Statistics (2019) Homicide in England and Wales: year ending March 2018 (average taken over 10 years)

In the year ending March 2019, 1.6 million women experienced domestic abuse
Office for National Statistics (2019) Domestic abuse victim characteristics, England and Wales: year ending March 2019

Violence Against Women (Credit: amnesty.org.uk)

What do we mean by violence against women?

We follow the UN definition which describes violence against women as

'any act of gender-based violence that results in, or is likely to result in, physical, sexual or psychological harm or suffering to women, including threats of such acts, coercion or arbitrary deprivation of liberty, whether occurring in public or in private life.' UN Declaration on the Elimination of Violence Against Women

It's a human rights issue

Violence against women is both a consequence of and a cause of inequality between men and women. As well as being a health problem of epidemic proportions, it's also a human rights problem of equal severity. Depending on the violation, it can deprive a woman of

- her right to health and physical and mental integrity
- her right to be free from torture, inhuman and degrading treatment
- her right to life.

While those rights are enshrined in the Universal Declaration of Human Rights, there are also specific pieces of international legilsation that protect a woman's right to be free from violence.

- The UN <u>Convention on the Elimination of All Forms of Discrimination against Women (CEDAW)</u>, adopted by the UN General Assembly in 1979, defines how UN member states should define and act to stop discrimination against women.

- In 1993 the General Assembly passed the <u>Declaration on the Elimination of Violence Against Women (EVAW)</u> which recognised that violence against women is widespread, that it comes from a historically unequal relationship between men and women, and that it is used as a mechanism to subordinate women. The Declaration called on UN member states to work together to eliminate an issue that is 'an obstacle to the achievement of equality, development and peace'.

As a survivor, I can relate to the wealth of emotions that many victims may have ruminating in their heads, 24/7. Feelings of guilt, shame, loneliness, low self-esteem, or fear. More often than not, it is the very same person/people that you put your love and trust into who become the abuser/s. They feed off endearing elements of someone's personality – their kindness, their honesty, their empathy, their ability to show compassion and their air of vulnerability.

But why do abusers do this? What is their purpose or mission? It is part of their agenda to build a sense of trust with you, to create a sense of feeling safe in their presence. For when they have achieved this hidden agenda, the abuser will use this fake trust to control your daily life, from the moment you wake up until you go to bed at night.

Abusers formulate a clever persona which they showcase to the world to show how charming, intelligent, caring, or shy they are. The way that I prefer to describe this to women who connect with me is that abusers are a wolf in sheep's clothing; Matthew 7:15 King James Version (KJV) *Beware of false prophets, which come to you in sheep's clothing, but inwardly they are ravening wolves. (biblegateway.com)*

The purpose of compiling this book is to raise awareness of the signs of domestic violence and abuse and, in turn, offer hope, empowerment, support, and inspiration to other women by letting them know that they are not alone in their suffering. There are millions of women around the world who are walking in the same shoes – shoes that fit yet are unbearable to wear. For they are the shoes of intelligent, kind, worthy, strong, resilient women who are striving to walk in shoes of freedom.

Protest about the Family Courts

Parliament Square, London October 2019

Why should any of us have or need to conform to what our family, friends or society expects from us when we are the ones living in fear, despair and anguish every day? It is our life, our emotional and physical wellbeing that is being punished at the hands of another human being.

I was always too scared to speak up to anyone, always fearing the worst. But now I have reinvented myself into the woman I have always wanted to be. The events happening in my life right now are truly amazing and give me the motivation I need to continue my quest to help other women and young girls.

I would like to say a huge thank you to all the supporters of the Crowdfunder Campaign that I organised in February 2020 for 5 weeks, and also to those individuals who donated via PayPal. It is because of your generosity and human kindness that this book has been able to grow from a typed manuscript into a published book. I would not have been able to complete the compilation and publication without your very kind donations. This book is a testament to what it is to be human. To reach out to each other in times of crisis and suffering – to offer a listening ear and an intangible hug of reassurance.

I would also like to thank Dr Miriam Dalli MEP for her continued support over the past two years and for endorsing this book. I am a very happy woman!

Last, but by no means least. Thank you to my wonderful children for just being who you are and for fulfilling my life with so much joy, love and laughter.

COVID-19

&

Coercive Control

The Hidden Epidemic

Where do I even begin with this chapter? Who knew our daily lives, our world, would be turned upside-down by an inanimate object? An object that cannot be seen with the human eye, a virus with a diameter of approximately 125 nanometres? (Credit: National Centre for Biotechnology Information). Invisible to the human eye, yet devastatingly visible when the novel virus hijacks a 'host'. One world in a stake of shock, one word on everyone's lips – coronavirus.

In the midst of chaos, confusion, fear, and uncertainty, we have all become accustomed to a new way of living, encompassing new terms we have never heard of, yet they have imminently become a part of our vocabulary - Self-isolating; Quarantine; Covid-19; Social Distancing; Flatten The Curve? But have you heard these terms before? Coercive Control? Intimate Partner Abuse? Power & Control Wheel? Coercive Behaviour? During a time in our lives when the whole world is facing one of its biggest ever challenges since WWII, a battle not being fought with infantry weapons, naval ships, and fighter planes.

I believe that this war is far more destructive. The enemy is known, yet it travels indiscriminately from one continent to another, desperately seeking a host cell to transmit its genetic material. The novel coronavirus, and all other viruses, can only proliferate by passing on their genetic code to a living cell. Viruses are not classed as living organisms as they cannot metabolize on their own or possess a cell membrane, unlike our human cells. I can remember this scientifc information from when I was a mature student at the University of Greenwich in 2009 whilst studying for a Foundation Degree in Biomedical Science. At that time, it was one of my dreams to become a Biomedical Scientist. I love to challenge myself to see what I am capable of achieving. Sadly, I was unable to complete my Degree due to unforeseen circumstances, but I still enjoy learning new courses on the free educational website, FutureLearn.com (in collaboration with The Open University).

If this global health and economic crisis isn't enough for us all to comprehend and cope with – it is truly heartbreaking to read in national newspapers in the UK that there has been a 25% increase in the number of phone calls and online requests for help, as reported by The National Domestic Abuse helpline on behalf of the charity, Refuge. Women and children are living in a toxic environment, constantly walking on eggshells so as not to upset the abuser.

To live in their own homes, which should be THEIR sanctuary, and yet, it has become their prison cell.

Women and children fearing for their lives, not just because of this global pandemic and the potential threat it poses to every human being, but very tragically because victims of domestic violence are living with a hidden epidemic.

From dawn to dusk, victims are desperately trying to survive. Constantly seeking to appease their abuser, to get through breakfast with the hope that they will survive till lunchtime, dinner, bedtime. Perpetrators have NO excuse for their abhorrent behaviour. There is NEVER an excuse for physical, emotional, or sexual abuse.

Whilst Lockdown continues in the UK (as at the time of writing this chapter, 30th April 2020), and around the world, victims of domestic violence are far more vulnerable, isolated, fearful, and lonely, more now than they ever were. Can you imagine how that must feel? To know that if you tried to make an escape and flee your home – your initial thoughts would be 'who/what would get me first … my partner or the coronavirus'?. How many women right now are frantically running around their home to find their mobile, because their landline has been broken? How many women are trying to get access to a laptop to log on to a domestic violence organisation to seek help? How many women are trying desperately to protect their children from harm, and in doing so, are enduring the violent wrath of their abuser?

Perpetrators patrolling the household, intentionally using gaslighting techniques to manipulate their victim, at any cost, just so they can gain control.

POWER & CONTROL WHEEL

How To Stay Safe

• Try to make contact with local charities, via email, phone, WebChat, social media group, or by asking a trusted member of the family or friend. Call the Police in an emergency and even if you are unable to talk, leave the phone line 'open'.

• Set up a special word for you and your children – one which will enable you to put together a plan to leave the household.

• Keep your mobile charged all the times and, if possible, keep a back-up one – any old phone that you can use to make a phone call.

• Find out about what APPS are available to download in order to help protect you and provide the information you need to stay safe.

• Don't ever feel ashamed, embarrassed, guilty, or too blame for the horrors you are going through. Abuse is NOT your fault. Perpetrators are weak and insecure, and therefore, seek to break the spirits of strong, confident, intelligent women who know their worth. It is YOUR strength of character that is enabling you and your children to exist.

For me, living in lockdown has resurfaced so many emotions from my past and present – emotions that cause constant ruminations where my mind is fleeting from one painful memory to the next, as if it's on a loop. Emotions don't care what time of the day it is, or where you are, who you are with, or how it will make you feel. Your mind needs to find the space and time to process these emotions, to make sense of them and to realise that you are in control. You have the power to practice mindfulness, yoga, talk therapy, etc. To formulate a plan to deal with your thoughts as and when they arise, and how best to overcome them. The brain is a very powerful tool, and as you know, traumatic experiences can have devastating effects on you mentally and physically.

I was diagnosed with PTSD in 2013, and even though this diagnosis upset me, it also helped me to realise that the symptoms I had been experiencing was attributed to a well-known medical condition, and I wasn't going mad (as some people assumed). The sad fact about living with PTSD is that many people then go on to develop Fibromyalgia, which is a long-term condition that causes generalised pain across the body, as well as other symptoms. I developed Fibromyalgia in 2015, and there were times when the pain was so bad I needed to use a walking stick to do the school run or go for a walk.

Please remember this, this bravest thing you could ever do is ask for help. For this is the biggest step you can take towards a better life. Never feel ashamed of how you feel and never listen to those individuals who mock you when you disclose personal information about your symptoms. Reach out to someone you can trust and begin your journey of healing.

There will be a time shortly when governments around the world will be in a position to relax some of the current restrictions, and we will all be able to start socialising again, and to return to some degree of normal, a new normal. But think for one minute right now about how your daily life is going to change after self-isolating and lockdown? For you, it could be the start of a new chapter in your life, with a new sense of self and compassion. Some women may find the courage to go back to work or to seek gainful employment; some women will be able to find an escape from the horrors of their home life, simply by being able to do the school run every day; some women may have their mobile phones returned back to them by their abuser; some women will may feel strong enough to leave the confines of their home whilst their abuser is out of the house.

Young girls and women and around the world should be living their lives **without** fear, isolation, pain, or suicidal ideation due to enduring emotional and/or physical violence.

For victims of domestic violence, daily life after weeks of self-isolation evolves back into isolation - the same traumas – different day.

We are entitled to our freedom

To be treated equally

To be independent

To be treated fairly and with respect

Chapter 1

Lisa Edwards

Lisa A. Edwards & Skipper Doodle

165 Johnston Street Unit #2
Newburgh, NY 12550
Phone: USA 914-505-5451-mobile

LifestyletoIndependence.com
Lisa-A-Edwards.com/Pubic Speaking

LisaE@Lifestyletoindependence.com e-mail

 Lifestyle to Independence

 Lisa A Edwards

 @LisaAEdwards1

Lisa has been a voice for others that suffer from domestic violence since joining Toastmasters International in 2008, and in 2014 becoming an Independent Certified Speaker, Teacher, and Coach with the John Maxwell Team. Lisa, along with her dog Skipper Doodle, serve as the face of a small company with a big mission. Lisa founded two Social Entrepreneurial Companies, 2016 Lifestyle to Independence/Developer of affordable housing & 2018 LTI Company/Public Speaking & Product Development. Once a victim, now a survivor, Lisa shares her inspirational message of hope and a roadmap to financial independence in supporting female veterans and domestic violence survivors.

The Astonishing Power of Hope by Lisa Edwards

When I was a little girl, I had such an amazing free spirit and I just loved life. Have you ever felt or believed that you were destined to do something very, very, special? Well, I did!

At the tender age of 13, my world came crashing down around me. My most important influencers in my life were calling it quits and my father had left our *home sweet home*. Like a little puppy following its owner, I was my father's shadow and now I had no one to follow. I was lost, felt abandoned, lonely, and most of all I didn't know how much that permeated my inner voice, and would affect my life's decisions. Come to think of it, my outer side didn't seem to match my inner side, although, no one could tell, not even me.

My Olympic dreams had come to a crashing halt, since we no longer could afford private lessons, or afford anything else for that matter, including the necessities of life. My saving grace was standing on my head or flipping upside down, it gave me something to focus on, something to look forward to. With total concentration and repetition, my brain commanded my body to move in unrealistic ways. I learned about discipline, dedication, and not being on my feet, which brought me such joy, 6 days a week, 9 months a year. It was something that I was good at, it was something to look forward to. Most importantly, it gave me hope through my teenage years. I guess I would say it was my Teacher, helping me get through the tough times, and keeping my mind focused. Being a gymnast, little did I know how important those lessons would serve me later in life.

Well, I have a new dream and I'm excited to share it with you, but first, let me tell you how I found my way. In the last 22 years, I lost 7 homes, 4 jobs, 2 cars, and my son when he was 5 ½ years old on the second custody battle to an abusive ex-husband.

My abuser did not want to strangle me, nor shoot me. He said, "If you do as I say in my petition for divorce, you'll get more, if not, I promise to bury you alive. You'll never amount to anything, you're worthless, I'll make sure you're on welfare, just like when you were a teenager, and I'll take my son."

My ex's determination and mission in life was to elicit power and control, induce pain and fear, and bring harm to me in any way he could. To destroy my self-esteem, finances, relationships, and any dreams that I could ever dream of. Unfortunately, our son was his ultimate prize.

Besides the personal losses I endured, I was so abused, verbally, mentally, emotionally, physically, financially, sexually, and judicially. If there's another way, I don't want to know. So, what helped my abuser to accomplish his goals?

First, he became a leader of a Father's Rights group in Rockland County, NY. With all the support he could muster up, and besides not being in his own territory it was easier for him to tort the truth, rouse the troops, especially for his cause.

Secondly, he enlisted amazing support from a woman that he met in a local bar on his nightly happy hour. Suzanne soon became his girlfriend and hero, parading up and down the halls of Westchester Family Court engrossed 100% in all of his petitions including custody of our son, as a credible witness, so the Law Guardians agreed.

Thirdly, he took a Mediation Course at Westchester Family Court in NY. Understanding how the Family Court system works, he participated in the Domestic Violence program, taught by my Domestic Violence Advocate, Beverly Houghton. Beverly worked for The Office for Women in White Plains, NY. Subsequently, my OP was still current against my ex, and he learned how victims can stay safe and navigate the system.

My abuser was calculating and vicious and remaining in our 4-family home was nothing less than a daily and nightly struggle. When a victim is alone and isolated, you're an easier target. Staying in a safe and peaceful environment was something I would not experience for many years to come.

I remember being picked up and slammed onto a gravel driveway several times on my back. Everything was in slow motion; I was in such disbelief and shock. I didn't realize how bad the bruising and cuts were, well, not until I went to teach my water fitness class that week. Several of my students approached me after and I broke down. One woman drove me home and tried to help where she could. I visited a Judge from Peekskill, NY, and shared my story. He asked me, "Did you report this to the Police and get photos?" That would prove to be one of my worst mistakes. Regrettably, he was right, I filed for an OP in Family Court but I didn't do it soon enough.

My mother sent two airline tickets, so we could enjoy some time with her in sunny Florida. Seventy-five percent of our furniture was gone when we returned home. I was told that my son's belongings were also taken, although my soon-to-be ex-husband was advised that the Law Guardian would not take a liking to that. So he had to return them, as my lawyer explained.

One brisk Fall early morning, my son and I were taking a walk around our property. My soon-to-be ex-husband drove up in his truck and took Taylor. His truck door was open and I saw mail with my name on it. As I went to pick it up, he grabbed the mail from my hand and my keys, he walked firmly and directly towards the woods next to our house and threw my keys into the woods, so my son and I had no way to get in our home. He left me once again with his kind words, "You'll never have anything, so get used to it." This time I went back to court to file for the OP.

Having dinner with my son, I didn't realize his father was watching us, peering in our home window. I briefly left the room; he snatched our son from the dinner table, took him outside, put him in his swing, and continued to threaten me. I went over to the truck and started to carve into the side as I called the Police. They arrived, took the compliant, advised us that the truck belonged to both of us. That truck no longer came to my home again, that did not stop him.

Remember, every time a victim stands up for themselves there's always a price to pay. I didn't care. I was finally awarded a one-year OP, which gave me hope, hope that things would be a bit quieter.

Unfortunately, another tactical change, our son went on an extended visitation late one Friday afternoon. I returned home to find our television, phone, lights, and heat turned off by my soon-to-be ex-husband.

Help was not available till Monday and I had no way to communicate with our 2-year-old son. In addition, Suzanne, the Fiancée often made copies of our court documents to hand out like candy to our four tenants that lived above Taylor and me at our home.

The day I was forced out of our four-family home, I remember two events that happened that day. One, I was served petition papers for custody of our son, who was to attend kindergarten in a few days. Two, a Fed Ex truck arrived, and a package containing our 75-page divorce agreement was enclosed, my ex-husband's lawyer, who drew it up, nine months late. The lawyers fought over the content, I was forced out of my home along with my son, with no money, no job, no car, and no professional representation.

Within 30 days, I was able to hock some jewelry, including my engagement ring, get a loan from my friends, and rent a 1-bedroom attic apartment, land a travel job, defend myself in Westchester Family Court, and purchase a new car from my abusers' ex-best friend, who himself experienced Suzanne's playful side, pub hopping, and reckless behavior.

My ex was cheeky, bluntly reminding me that my OP for 4+ years was about to expire. He planted intimidating articles in our son's school bag, returning our son in full winter clothes, gloves covering his hands just to find out there were burns relating to a struggle with Suzanne whom Taylor was afraid of. Another time my son came back exhausted, quietly crying, and wanted to sleep with me. He clung to me and rested his head on my chest as I comforted him. He didn't want me to put him down for days. His face, hands, and nails were dirty and his clothes did not fit. When his face was cleaned of the dirt, his nose was bruised.

Unfortunately, once your child is returned from visitation and they disguise the issues, the emergency room has no proof of when or who caused the pain. My son would not speak to anyone, but me.

Living in the Westchester Family Court system for five full years, my abuser and his now-Fiancée, Suzanne, served petitions as often as possible. Their timing was precise and calculating, putting as much stress on my finances, my home, and, of course, my new job. I was also a Water Fitness Instructor and while I was teaching, my son attended the daycare center on the upper floor of the club. My ex had an OP against him, so he sent his Fiancée Suzanne, to drop in to see my son and to bring him things or give him a message. We were both feeling the stress and there were marked changes in my son, including excessive clingy behavior towards me, enuresis, and dropping his pants inappropriately at his daycare center.

I took my son to a Clinical Psychologist to see if he could help and we addressed the courts. Judge Adrienne Scancarelli ordered Psychiatric Evaluation to be conducted by Dr. Lawrence Loeb, for my son, myself, my ex, and his Fiancée Suzanne. In Dr. Loeb's finding of custody, he stated that "Residential custody should remain with the mother." Clearly, if the father was found to have been abusive, that would weigh most heavily in a custody determination. My abuser was losing this custody case, so he decided just not to show up. Years later, two lawyers reviewed all the case files and found those files went missing, including the Court Order from Judge Scancarelli for Dr. Lawrence Loeb's Psychiatric Evaluations. The two Lawyers wanted to know how I obtained those documents as proof. I explained, "I only share that information with the women I serve."

The situation escalated when my 4-year OP expired. The daring duo had me served with three petitions at my new job, one was for custody. Taking time off to defend myself put a tremendous strain on my clients I served and the agency I worked for. They thought it would be best if they fired me so I can collect unemployment while handling legal issues.

A Court-Appointed Lawyer was involved and there went my credibility. She was a close friend of my previous lawyer and removed herself from the case. The Honorable Adrienne Hofmann Scancarelli, Head Family Court Judge of Westchester County, NY, demanded of my advocate from The Office of Women, Beverly Houghton, that she no longer support my case in her courtroom. Through the Law Guardian on the case, my advocate was to call me and demand that I produce my son, or they would have me arrested. No Habeas Corpus, no legal representation, denied the ability to subpoena anyone including my advocate, Beverly Houghton.

36

My mother flew in from Fl, my boyfriend's father, who was an executive of his own successful company, sat by my side in the courtroom. The Judge gave temporary custody of our son to my ex-husband and his Fiancée without cause. They were also handed an OP against me for my son's and their safety. I was not granted any visitation rights. Part of the hearing seemed like it was in slow motion, as I repeated, "You're violating my civil rights," for the entire hearing. I felt like someone was trying to convince me that my perfectly healthy arm was gangrene as the judge ordered it to be chopped off with a guillotine. The executive sitting next to me stood up in the Courtroom yelling at the judge that there is no cause to take this child, no cause, several times. The executive said he no longer believes in the system and if he wasn't present, he would have never believed my story. The Judge advised me that I didn't deserve it but that she was going to give me a Court-Appointed Attorney for the Custody case, although the Lawyer would only be able to move forward.

I dropped off my 5-year-old son with my parents. We watched E.T. Go Home as our last movie together. He kissed his finger, touched his heart, and pointed at me, and said, "Ouch." Within 48 hours, my ex and his credible Fiancée as the Law Guardians agreed, filed papers to have me arrested and in jail.

Judge Scancarelli continued to pull me back to court to pay for my ex-husband's petition for custody for six months. One day, I was 15 minutes late in five years and Judge Scancarelli had a warrant out for my arrest. I was handcuffed and put in a cell for four hours, the Judge wanted to know the reason for my tardiness. I replied, "Due to the inclement weather, your Honor, the rain, sleet, and snow, the public transportation was 15 minutes late."

The Coalition for Family Justice was by my side on Dec 9, 1998, at 9:30 am. I was the first to see Judge Scancarelli on her last day. Once again, the Judge asked me if I was prepared to pay something toward the cost of the custody hearings that my ex-husband initiated, and I replied, "Unfortunately, I'm sorry to tell you besides losing my son I have also lost my job, my home, my car and right now I don't have any money to pay you." The Judge advised me that she would have the bills paid and I was excused. As I proceeded toward the doors, the Judge called out my name and as I turned, she said, "I'm truly sorry for your losses. I truly, truly am." I never responded.

I was not the only victim of her abuse. Judge Scancarelli continually worked with Forensic Psychologist, Melvin Sinowitz of Hartsdale, NY, who lost his license, credibility and was fined $5,000. There were plenty of victims and Beverly Houghton was one of them too. Domestic violence is a crime and the system is broken.

As for me, when I went to leave the courthouse, the ladies from the coalition gave me a birthday card with $50.00 and I was so touched. I left Westchester Family Court right before my 38th birthday, with my card, my $50.00, and the clothes on my back. You see, Judge Scancarelli has been dead for some time now, so I feel a little bit safer in telling my story.

Most difficult decision...

Shortly after the system failed for me and my son, I received a call. It was a recording and if I wanted to continue, I was to press number 7. This call was the shock of my life. It was an organization out of Atlanta, Georgia that helps to give a new life to a parent and their children once the system has failed. I've heard of such a thing, seen it in the movies, but they were calling me. I received their application in the mail and sat on my kitchen floor, crying, for three days. I knew the relief that I so desperately wanted for both my son and I. There was no fairness in our lives, I had nothing to lose. I thought of four reasons why I chose not to fill out the application in its entirety and mail it in. One, the abuser felt back in control, he felt he won the prize and he accomplished his goal for the time being. I felt my son was going to be less torn apart emotionally even though he was kept from me which was heart-wrenching. Second, if my son or I should need medical attention from a hospital, I would go directly to jail for kidnapping. Third, I dreamt of a healthy adult relationship with my son. Fourth is why I'm sharing my story. I pledged to God that if he helped me through this, I would be a voice for so many other women and children.

Along this journey, I was incarcerated three times before I went into hiding for about 1 ½ years. My abuser's next tactic was indigency. My ex filed for child support three times, twice when I was unemployed. And the third time his efforts prevailed because I was making more than the poverty level. I was now paying him and lost my safe room in hiding.

My girlfriend, Juanita, a Mary Kay Rep, gave me her first microloan for $165.00. Surrounded by loving, caring, positive women, I paid her $5.00 per month and zero interest. I'm sure my abusive ex-husband would never want anyone to know this, nonetheless, he enlisted support from a woman to attend one of my in-home beauty parties for his own financial gain. His constant abuse, beratement, and detectives following my every step was only a story you would see in the movies.

A short while after my-ex and his credible wife, Suzanne, as the Law Guardians agreed, turned on each other like vicious animals, sniffing out any opportunity to outdo one another. Putting me and my son in the middle and using him as a pawn. The local police department had files 5-6 inches high on the domestic abuse calls to their home. One report included my ex-husband chasing his stepchildren with broken beer bottles. My ex-husband had just called me the prior week advising me that he, Taylor, and his wife were moving upstate and if I did not cooperate, he would come after me financially.

Suzanne was telling me that her husband, my ex, explained that he had the right to have sex with her at any time, so she purchased a gun to protect herself. As a truly concerned stepmother, she was making sure I was well aware of the abuse my ex-husband handed out on a daily, if not hourly basis to all of them.

The court was a three-ring circus with Suzanne, me, and my ex. The new Judge was extremely concerned about my ex and forbade him to move. We had another court appearance for all of us, instead, I was called to my lawyer's office as he apologized to me. Suzanne will no longer be showing up at court because credible witnesses, as the Law Guardians agreed, was married to two men at the same time.

My ex, acting as pro se, went through Family Court because I was $920.00 in arrears/past due in child support and took my last $800.00 from my Putnam County Savings Bank and I was unable to pay my rent. My son was gone, my apartment was gone, I got in my car and drove to the Putnam County Hospital and stayed for three weeks, so I could find hope again.

My son once told me, "I have Suzanne to thank. It's because of her that I'm as strong as I am today." I told my son, "I have your father to thank. It's because of him that I'm as strong as I am today." And for that, I have nothing but pure Hope.

- 2009 I achieved the "American Dream," a home of my own and a brand-new start.
- 2016 I founded Lifestyle to Independence – Developer for Affordable Housing

- 2018 I founded LTI Company – Public Speaking Product Development.

Our mission is to strive to empower single female veterans and single domestic violence survivors by equipping each woman with the necessary tools and resources to lift themselves up from poverty to prosperity. We provide affordable, basic necessities of life, housing, food, and clothing. Lifestyle to Independence believes that everyone deserves a safe home to live, grow, and heal.

My dreams have become my reality, at Lifestyle to Independence we're not only in the business of building homes, but we're also in the business of rebuilding lives. Now we're reaching out to you and our communities to be part of the solution! Call or Email, let's connect and collaborate in equipping you and other women around the world.

With gratitude, Lisa E & Skipper Doodle

Chapter 2

Survivor

Overcoming Fear and Anxiety

When you hear domestic abuse, you probably think of a person beating their significant other. And when you read about domestic abuse, you hear about that victim's account 90% of the time. But something I don't often see is the accounts of the children in those situations. I don't know if it's because we remove ourselves as a victim in those situations or if it's for some other reason; some just don't remember because they were so young. But I do remember and I don't want to stay silent.

My parents had me before they were married, which is completely normal, but my father used me to manipulate my mother into marriage. And they both used me as an excuse to stay together for eleven years of my life. They then continued to use me as a means to get information, an outlet for their complaints about one another and to manipulate me to hate the other. Only recently, due to me removing my father from my life, have I gained any sort of peace regarding my family life.

As I grew from a baby to a pre-teen, I watched and was involved in intense stages of war and peace. I remember my mother disappearing, after hearing both of my parents screaming and arguing, to what I now know was a psychiatric ward or hospital. This is when my father invoked some of my more traumatic memories. He told me he was going to take me to see my mother, drove me around for what felt like the entire day or most of it, bought me a slice of pizza, and took me back home. We never stopped anywhere but for that singular slice and gas. My father used that time against my mother for the rest of their marriage and even after.

Then there was peace until my father used my asking him to leave my room so I could change after Halloween, to make me feel bad for him working and for his relationship with my mom. At age five or six, I had to hold and console my father over the fights he had with my mother over him not taking responsibility for the awful things he had done and said to my mother.

After more peace and more war, one of my parents' biggest fights took place. My father broke my mother's phone to prevent her from calling the police and my mother pushed my father out of the back door of our home, locking him out after loud screaming. Peace again, then after two emotional moves, my parents began constantly fighting. This is when my anxiety and depression began manifesting itself.

I began waking up in the middle of the night, hearing my parents screaming at each other. I would lay there crying, jumping at every loud noise, and begging for my mother to leave for work so the screaming would stop. They never hit each other, but their words were evil. I had my first ever anxiety attack at age eleven because of these early morning screaming matches and still cannot handle loud yelling of any sort without anxiety symptoms.

Then my mother began coming home from work and disappearing almost immediately to a friend's' house until late at night. It didn't take long for her to force me to meet her friend by picking me up from a friend's house in my hometown. I had a bad feeling about this man from the moment I saw him, and I would find out, over and over again later, why. My mother stopped to drop him off on our way home that night she had me meet him and made me wait in the car in the dark in a bad area of town, as a young child, for over thirty minutes. She had left her phone in the car and so I had opened it to see if maybe I could call the man she had gone inside with to get her to come down. And that was when I discovered my mother was cheating on my father. After that night, I didn't trust my mother and I never fully have for more reasons than this.

During this time, my mother and I fought a lot. This was the first time I can actually remember my mother choosing other things over being a mother. And that's not me being upset because my mother wanted some sort of life outside of parenting - that's normal. She chose to be almost non-existent in my life for almost six months during some of the hardest years of my life.

One of the only conversations I can remember from that time, and I shouldn't even call it a conversation, was when she told me that it didn't matter how I felt because my emotions weren't real. That they were made up in my head and that I needed to get over myself and stop blaming other people for my issues. This was in response to me crying and shaking and being upset after she walked towards me as if she was going to hit me. Regardless of whether or not she was going to, she used actions that my mind had previously seen and perceived as how someone acts when they want to harm someone else and my mind reacted to that. And instead of handling it like the adult in the scenario, she forced all the blame onto me and then disappeared back to her friend's house.

Six months after discovering my mother cheating, after countless nights of their screaming, and me having anxiety attacks up in my room, my father announced that they were getting a divorce, which was extremely devastating for me. I had constantly been told growing up that I was the only reason they got married and so in my head at that time, I was the reason for the divorce even though there were a million viable variables in place to cause this to happen. And while I'm old enough to understand that they can't put their choice to marry each other on me, their decision to marry based on bringing my life into this world was selfish. Children aren't a puzzle piece you can use to glue pieces back together, they are humans developing their own emotions and you are supposed to be their glue.

When he told my sister and me, I immediately went to the barn. Horses have been a constant safety net in my life. I have been around them since I was three or four and have ridden since I was five or six and have always been a barn rat. When I was a kid, I was always at the barn, and now that I'm an adult I realize, other than when my mother took me along to her barn jobs, it was a way to get away from everything at my house. Especially when the divorce was happening. I didn't want to be around the fighting and my parents used me as much as they could to figure out information about each other. This was also when I began to write a lot, writing about other worlds seemed much more appealing than living on my own at the time.

During the divorce, my father began the manipulation game. He had always made my mother and her mental illness seem way worse than they actually were. He had told me my mother had schizophrenia multiple times in my childhood and once the divorce began, he tried to say that the court could use that against her if they found out. He also refused to move out of the house he agreed we could stay in just because he couldn't be bothered to find a new garage to put his items in. This put my mother in an extremely tough financial situation and he tried to avoid paying child support because he struggled with money due to refusing to leave the house he couldn't afford to live in. Luckily, the judge fixed that quickly and made him pay the correct amount and the divorce was finalized and over.

For a solid five seconds, I had relief. No more arguments, no more screaming and arguing. Things would calm down. But this is when things became bad again. My father would drive me to school each day and would try to get me to talk about my mother. My mother would constantly say horrible things about my dad to me and would call him gay for having male friends. She had also invited her friend to live with us and I had to begin to listen to racist, sexist, homophobic rhetoric from this man. He hung a Confederate flag in his garage and tried to argue that the Civil War had nothing to do with slavery.

After he moved in, I discovered he was a convict. He also would shoot up heroin or crack, I'm not sure which, but they are equally bad and he would constantly drive while under the influence of drugs and alcohol. I later found out that he had previously beaten his dog for normal canine behavior. He never made any sort of effort to be a healthy part of mine or my sister's life and would get upset that we didn't like him due to his behavior.

My mother also acted racist, trying to defend the 'N' word to me after me not being okay with her using it. She would call my father gay because he had other male friends, knowing I was a part of the LGBTQ community. And she would gaslight me and say I was the one causing the issue when I would get upset about this and more.

At this time, I dealt with it and brushed almost everything he did off my shoulder because I knew my dad wasn't good for me. I was distancing myself from him and didn't want to push my mother away either. I was also naive and didn't realize he was abusive towards my mother. I was so use to the family hiding things and not making a big deal out of these things that I didn't fully realize how harmful he was truly being. I was also used to my father's specific manipulation abuse that this was almost foreign to me in a way.

I began realizing, for good, that he wasn't a good person after he pulled a loaded gun on my mother in front of me. I heard arguing so I went outside where my mother and he were at the time, and my mother told me to go back inside as he had a gun pointed at her. I went inside and through the front door to the neighbors and waited for my mom there, terrified as I heard him shooting it around. I still wish I had called the Police that day, but both my mother and he scared me out of doing so.

Throughout the rest of my teenage years, he did many horrible things to my mom and they broke up multiple times, once making us move in the process, because of him doing the same abusive things over and over. He continuously lost jobs due to attacking other co-workers, bullying other co-workers, not doing his job properly, and probably more that I can't think of. He consistently made my mother think she was the one at fault for being upset over him not helping around the house, not doing the things he said he would do, and recently, having to manage his medicine for him.

By eighteen, I made the choice to not have my father in my life any longer. I told him why and he turned everything I said around on me. He is blocked on every platform I'm active on and has no place in my future for the time being. I've told him what he needs to do to come back into my life and, so far, not only has he refused to do so, but he has acted as if nothing has ever happened or, when asked about it, as if it's all my fault. I love my father, but I don't have to be around his manipulative abuse to know that he has a place in my heart. I don't think I would've chosen to disconnect from him like I did if I hadn't met my boyfriend who introduced me to some of the first truly healthy relationships of my life. His actions made me realize that healthy relationships don't involve manipulation and he has been a rock for me in that regard since I met him.

Since removing my father from my life, I've had to build a lot of myself back up. The hardest thing after coming out of a childhood of trauma is figuring out who you actually are. Your life becomes filled with guards around every corner and in places that make no sense. You have fears and anxieties about things that you know you shouldn't worry about in the slightest. Your senses kick into overdrive over the most normal things and, especially for me, you have a hard time making and keeping friends. And those are really hard challenges to overcome. My brain still struggles with putting the walls away and I don't know if they will ever fully crumble.

However, I'm pushing past all of these things. I've created healthy hobbies and passions, I've figured out ways to release my pent-up emotions and memories and, while I'm still figuring it out with therapy and other things, I feel like I'm slowly getting to a healthier place.

A lot of the things I've chosen to surround myself with have been chosen with care and really help me grow and releases me from my depression and anxiety. I nanny and babysit and have an incredible passion for helping and advocating for children. I put my heart and soul into my job as a nanny because I want to see these children grow in a healthy environment where they can prosper. That may be a coping and healing mechanism but if I'm able to help children while doing it, I'm on the right path.

I'm also very much into house plants and animals and I want to get into creating my own aquariums that filter themselves with aquatic plants and cleaner crew animals. I also plan on getting rodents, most likely gerbils. Surrounding myself with nature and animals has increased my happiness one hundred percent and has helped me realize that I want to either Major in botany or zoology in the future. It also allowed me to discover my true passion in life.

I have worked really hard to become independent and hope to be fully so by the time you turn these pages. Both of my parents have made it abundantly clear that I'm a burden to them and I don't need the emotional battle between either of them or my own brain. My mother most recently made this abundantly clear after throwing a tantrum about me not having time yet to place a phone call, when I still had plenty of time before the deadline for a call, to switch a payment over to my own account. She gaslighted me and told me I was acting like my father, which I was not, when I would not put up with her belittling me and with her making me feel like I was a financial burden on the people who chose to have me. I won't be the replacement for her to argue with just because she chose to divorce my father.

So, I really focus on positive relationships and I am very careful about who I let in. And people don't get second chances as much anymore because doing so has caused more pain than growth. Not to say people don't get them, but I don't hand them out as freely as I once did.

I've also recently focused on learning to stand up for myself professionally and positively. I used to get really defensive and a bit mean when people were mean to me first and I don't want to continue life feeling like I'm battling people. I want to say the truth in a healthy way, not give in to the negativity. And a lot of that has come from my recent studies of the Wiccan religion which I decided to join.

The Wiccan faith is a nature-based religion, which is already something I always felt a strong pull or connection to. I also strongly agree with its fundamental rules and beliefs on the afterlife, and finally, felt a connection to the religion in a way I never thought possible. I've felt great peace during my studies and practice and I've noticed a change in my outlook on life since becoming Wiccan. I believe that the Wiccan faith is the final step in what I needed to begin a full path to healing. Not to say there won't be smaller things along the way to help my path, but I do believe it will be the largest for a long while.

Healing is a never-ending journey. The pain goes away for the most part, but there will always be a little piece of it left to occasionally hurt. I have questions that will go unanswered for the rest of my life and plenty of things that I will never get the chance to say due to their unwillingness to listen. My parents used each other as ways to release anger and when they couldn't take that frustration out on each other, they used me instead. My only hope is that my story helps someone who went through what I did. And that those who have gone through what I have find peace in their lives.

Chapter 3
Ann Marina Longstaff

Ann Marina Longstaff has suffered long term from c-PTSD and other delicate mental health issues, which remained undiagnosed and misunderstood until she was 60 years old! This has led to difficulties in achieving personal goals and fulfilling her life's potential.

She lives a quiet life in the pretty seaside town of Hythe, Kent (England) with partner Andy and English Setters Lulu, Stormie, Shadow, and Rainbow. Ann Marina loves dogs and other animals with kindness, gentleness and respect.

This is the first time she has written anything for publication. Her writing comes straight from the heart, showing emotions and fears running very deep.

Email: annmarina@yahoo.com

Facebook: Ann Marina Longstaff

To Be Treasured

My twin and I were born seven weeks early in December 1957. A priest read the Last Rites to us. Two days old, Marina died. I was in the hospital for eleven weeks, but with a healthy beating heart and fighting spirit Little Ann survived. Being a lone twin has instilled a deep belief in me that life is a beautiful gift to be treasured. (I have added Marina to my name, in memory of my twin.)

Family life was happy, though we rarely had luxuries. Dad had been seriously injured in an army training exercise during the war. Physically, he lost a leg and the use of one arm. Emotionally and psychologically, he lost so much more. I understand that now. It's amazing how he coped.

Growing up, children of all ages played together out in the street - tag, hide and seek, hopscotch, and in our nearby woods we made camps, picked bluebells, climbed trees, and scraped our knees. Autumn, we played conkers, no gloves, no goggles - and even survived to tell the tale!!

Dad had a disability car, designed for one-person use. It was our family car!!   We sat one in front of the other in the side storage space. To balance the car out, shopping and one brother sat in the opposite, very narrow space. (Luckily we were all skinny). When dad spotted a police car, he would give the warning for us all to duck. People must have thought it was a TARDIS when they saw us all getting in and out. I have treasured memories of family from those simple, uncomplicated times.

Being openly kind, trusting, and caring, I naturally chose to surround myself with people who held similar values. Sadly, my empathy has made me a sitting target for manipulators who thrive on relentlessly using abusive or coercive fear to weaken, punish, and hurt a gentle soul. They are like the Dementors from the Harry Potter films, who drain every drop of happiness and energy from their victims. There's always one lurking in the shadows, waiting for their turn with me. It's a game for them.

1967 Aged 9. My innocent view of the world was challenged during a visit to a park. My friend and I were tricked into going with a stranger, with the promise of seeing some kittens. He led us along an isolated path, made us pull our pants down, and lift our dresses to waist height. We had to step forwards, closer to him while he dropped his trousers and did something disgusting to himself. My friend escaped around the corner and, alone with him, I was frozen with fear. Then we ran and his voice followed us, "Look what you've just done, you naughty, dirty little girls", and he threatened to come and find us if we told anyone.

I've always convinced myself (and felt relieved) that we got off lightly because I'm sure he didn't actually touch us. But I do remember feeling a sudden stabbing pain in my stomach. It had me doubled over just before I escaped, and I've never been able to make sense of this.

During Cognitive Behavioural Therapy (CBT), some fifty years later, I recalled becoming frightened of my darling Dad after what happened with the man in the park. I avoided being in the same room with him and couldn't look at him without seeing the man there in front of me. I still feel terrible that I never told him why. Family life changed forever when Dad died of a sudden massive heart attack in 1971. He was only 47 years old.

The following, just the tip of the iceberg.

Age 20, I met someone, fell in love and we got engaged. But through the love blindness, I couldn't see I had been deliberately targeted. He became the ruler of my world so quickly. He shredded everything about me into tiny pieces and stamped his own name on it all. I don't even know how I let it happen. I had been so ambitious and independent before I met him, following my dream of working in dog breeding kennels, with show dogs.

He was an opportunist thief and things were always going missing from our family home. He stole a silver charm bracelet, which was a 21st birthday gift from my best friend, Mandy. It was loose-fitting on my wrist so he convinced me it must have slipped off. He took my dance competition photo album and never returned it. When I asked for it back again, he ignored me. Complete silence. Why?

When I went out for the day to Cruft's Dog Show I received the sulky, silent treatment on my return. Mum was so uncomfortable with the way he had just turned up, hours before I was due home.

And there he was waiting, rattling those symbolic, though very effective, jailers' keys at me.

Just before Christmas, we exchanged gifts to open with our families on the big day. I'd given him some lovely things. He produced a small oblong package for me and hinted there was something special inside. I guessed it may be a pretty bracelet to replace the one I had 'lost' a few months earlier.   Excitement turned to tears on Christmas morning, when I opened it to find the smallest, cheapest box of chocolates imaginable (Matchmakers). I noticed the shock on the faces of my mum and brothers, all sickened by his deliberate cruelty. I didn't want them to see how bitterly upset and disappointed I was feeling and went upstairs to my room for a good cry.

He was physically and sexually violent. He raped me and silenced me with more violent threats and even made light of his actions by saying it was more fun and exciting to do it like that. (It was no fun having his hand on my throat and seeing the non-human, glazed look in his eyes). The game of minds he played had him constantly switching personas from the cold, manipulative rapist, to the Mr. Nice Guy, who sometimes showed an almost boyish excitement at wanting to marry me.

He asked me to go fishing with him and to sleep together overnight in his tent. When I told Mum, she looked worried. She had tried to coax me into opening up to her a few days earlier but I couldn't break my silence, even though she had noticed obvious bruising on me. I was of two minds about going but knew he would be angry if I didn't turn up as planned.

I arrived there mid-evening, excited with the news that I had been looking at wedding dresses with my bridesmaid. He poured me a cup of tea and I noticed him putting whiskey in it, so I accidentally spilled the tea. There was a camera set up. Two of his friends were in a nearby tent. He went to talk to them and I overheard heard him saying, "She's a bit shy, but you will be able to meet her later when she's nice and relaxed". It was getting dark now. I felt panicky, out of my depth. I thought of making a run for it, but this seemed a hopeless idea as I was so far from safety.

Then I heard the voice of an absolute angel – Mum, with my brothers, calling me from the pathway. She demanded answers from him to the lies, theft, fake wedding plans, and those bruises. He didn't know where to look or what to say, true colours finally revealed. Relieved, shocked, and devastated, all in one huge emotion, and completely overwhelmed, I fell to the floor and threw up.

All along I had been in desperate denial, making wedding plans. How could he do that, pretend to love me, but hate me? The truth is it broke me, and the truth was so painful that for years I hid it behind layer upon layer of happy smiles. Writing this has helped me face the reality of what he did to me, and much of the negative energy that's been trapped inside me from him has finally been released.

Hythe held too many memories. I went fifty miles away to work at Northgate Gundogs, a boarding and breeding kennel. It was an idyllic, happy escape, helping to care for more than thirty beautiful English Setters, adult dogs, and puppies.

In 1982, I met a new boyfriend. He had such a happy go lucky personality, always the life and soul of the party. He made me laugh so much and I loved this side of him.   In stark contrast, he could suddenly get angry with his mum and sister. This shocked me as it seemed so out of character. It must have been hard work, keeping up the nice guy pretence with me until we were married.

He had a knack of making comments that seemed quite normal or funny on the surface but carried confusing or hurtful undertones. Then, if upset, I would be accused of overreacting or told I had no sense of humour. It didn't take much for his anger to boil over. Anything from overspending on the food shopping, moving or touching his belongings, or adding the wrong sauce to his pasta! He would pace up and down, bang his fists hard on the table, shout and swear close up to my face. His favourite shout was, "This is my house, my mortgage. YOU do as I say"!!

When we visited my family or friends, he always got himself in a complete rage for the entire journey, whilst driving erratically. I would arrive emotionally drained, almost in tears, and in totally the wrong frame of mind to be sociable. And yet once out of the car, his change of mood into Mr. Happy was instant. I'm sure he had a built-in on/off switch!! He crashed the car once and it was more luck than judgment that no one was seriously injured.

I had to agree with his opinions, and if I had different ideas he took my voice away from me by drowning it out with his own louder voice. Always ridiculed for having any of my own interests and bullied into giving them up.

In 2010, three months before our 25th wedding anniversary, I left him. I'd planned my exit secretly without saying a word to him. If I had dared to ask for a divorce he would have shut me down completely and made it impossible for me to leave. I was granted a divorce on the grounds of his unreasonable behaviour. He never hit me, all the damage was caused by his intense and volatile anger, constant emotional abuse, and fears that he may one day completely lose control during one of his rages. I was constantly on edge and in a state of vigilance. A week or so before leaving, I asked "Whatever I say or do, I am always in the wrong in your eyes. I don't know what to do anymore. Tell me what I need to do?" He said, "Why don't you try going and f*****g hanging yourself". I knew I had made the right decision!

After the divorce, I found the perfect little house to rent in Hythe, very close to where I had lived with my family. I began convincing myself I could see the ex-boyfriend almost everywhere. I actually saw his face and mannerisms in people, which brought back panic and fears of being raped again. Then, in November 2016, I began having disturbing flashbacks to a childhood sexual attack and this appeared as photo shots in my mind. I can only describe the flashback experience as being captured in a slow-motion scene of a movie. I was frightened of what these memories were showing me and

61

wished for it to go away and stop upsetting me. It refused to go away and I strongly believe the flashbacks have given me the missing jigsaw pieces to my life. Even though awful to see, they fit in and make perfect sense. The effect of it though has turned my world upside down.

I'm left with an empty void and anger that my future choices were taken away to satisfy someone's vile urges. For months, all I could think about was the attack and I still feel it's the only thing that defines who I am. I'm so angry that my personal choices, even my potential for the future, were stolen when I was too young to understand or cope. Now I'm left to pick up the pieces more than fifty years later. And the way I see myself? I honestly don't know who I am anymore. How could something so life-changing have been a lost memory for so many years?

Constant waves of deep, sad feelings, like when you remember a recent death and feel that sudden rushing pain of the bereavement pang. It is the worst feeling ever, like standing in a lift that suddenly drops right down to the basement. I will not take drugs for depression, preferring to ride the highs and lows to gently, slowly heal naturally, thoughts and feelings free, not suffocated.

A Consultant Psychiatrist helped me to understand. The childhood memory loss was a coping mechanism my brain used to protect me. (In my minds' eye, I had locked the abuse memory in a cartoon style thought bubble next to my head) His diagnosis was that I have Complex Post Traumatic Stress Disorder, severe, having been undiagnosed, misunderstood and unnoticed for years, and this has caused severe anxiety and fears of abandonment that run very deep. It's hard to understand all these things. I'm easily overwhelmed, stay home a lot, and can't cope with any stress or even small unexpected things in daily life, coping with it by seeking out peace, quiet, and solitude 99% of the time

Without a word, I silently backed off massively from life, family, friends, the world, simply because my head was too full and spinning with memories of past and present personal upsets, sadness, grief, abuse, and rejection. This was my time for the self-care and preservation of a (now sixty-two-year-old woman) who has never deliberately done anything to hurt anyone and is now learning the story of her frightened *inner child,* needing to know she's safe - the little girl and the grown-up woman together in mind and body. Mental health and abuse, people feel uncomfortable about it, so it's easier to keep quiet. Too upset to speak the words of my abuse out loud at counselling, I wrote it all out beforehand and gave it to them to read.

My partner, Andy, has been kind and patient, my lovely friends, new and old, we look out for each other and share empathy and kindness. We all have our problems. My beautiful dogs Lulu, Stormie, Shadow, and Rainbow, are all such gentle souls. When I'm unhappy, they cuddle into me and those soft dark eyes seem to mirror the sadness they see.

I applied for Personal Independence Payments, but my claim was rejected, even after taking it to the appeal courts. They tell me c-PTSD isn't severe enough! Now I worry about what will happen when

Andy's health worsens. He has Parkinson's disease. What if he's forced to give up working and we can't afford to keep our beautiful dogs together as a family?   With this in mind, I set up a fundraising project for them. They give so much unconditional love to us and I feel it's the least I can do for them.

The project, with GoFundMe, is called, 'Help Needed For My English Setter Family'

I would like to end my chapter on a light-hearted note with healthy mindsets to starve all Dementors of their energy, and magical spells that will send them right out of the dumble-door!!

Self Help Healing Magic Spells:

What spell will take away the anger when I think about past abuse?

• Remember I can't change the past because it has already happened. Instead, practice focusing on the moment.

• Fighting the past will only take away the present, which will become lost and wasted forever.

• Anger and resentment are like a hungry wolf. If I keep feeding it, I will just make it more powerful. Starve it!!

Repeat to myself the spell **EXPECTO PATRONUM** to help guard me against the harmful memories. In my mind's eye, I will create my Patronus – (a clear image of a sweet happy memory)

What spell will help me feel better when I'm depressed?

• Remember the feeling won't last forever. It will definitely pass.

• A quick fix tonic is to cuddle my dogs and be aware of their soft, kind, and loving faces.

I will use meditation to cast
the **CHEERING CHARM** upon myself and create feelings of contentment:

Sit or look outside. Notice the gentle sights and sounds of nature. Relax and take three long, deep breaths. Notice the natural rhythm of my breath as it enters and leaves my body. Be aware that I am breathing in positive life force energy from the universe, and with each out-breath, releasing emotional pain. Continue with this until I feel more at peace within myself.

What spell will help to calm anxiety, panic, and fear?

• Notice my senses of sight, hearing, touch, taste, and smell to take the attention away from how I'm feeling.

• Create a safe place in my mind and remember all the comforting things I have put there and I will visit this place whenever I need to.

Use the **OBLIVIATE SPELL** to destroy the fears or the **RIDDIKULUS SPELL** to transform them into something funny.

Stay safe. Take care of yourselves and each other.

Chapter 4

Gabrielle Spierer

Gabrielle Spierer, a native New Yorker, is the President of Out of the Box Services (O.T.B.) where she speaks, educates, and counsels people to help them be their authentic selves; overcome the effects of domestic violence, and break patterns of unhealthy behaviors and relationships. Gabrielle was a mechanical design engineer for 15 years and then worked at Newsday for 23 years, where in 2012-2013, she successfully transitioned on the job, retaining over 800 customers.

As a child of Holocaust victims, she's overcoming a lifetime of domestic violence, including bullying and extreme emotional and physical abuse. For most people, the journey to becoming their authentic selves is difficult enough, but for Gabrielle overcoming the effects of a non-supportive environment has turned out to be the more difficult journey.

During this journey, she's learned and experienced a lot about gender, people's behaviors, laws of attraction, trauma, bullying, and the importance of a supportive environment for an emotionally healthy life. She's presented workshops on Successfully Transitioning in the Workplace, The Importance of a Supportive Environment, Being Your Authentic Self, The Effects of Making Change on the Family, and Overcoming the Trauma of Childhood Bullying at many conferences and colleges.

In October 2019, Gabby was the Keynote speaker at Suffolk County LI's Commemoration Day event during Domestic Violence Awareness month. Gabrielle's on the board of numerous organizations including Long Island's Community Advisory Board, CAB for Northwell Health. In 2015, she went back to school for her social work degree and plans to write a book on her life. Gabrielle's most important job in life is overcoming the effects of her past relationships to build a healthy one with her son!

Gabrielle can be reached on her US phone number at (631) 857-2244

Email address is gabriellespierer@gmail.com

Facebook account is Gabrielle Spierer

Twitter account is @GabrielleSpier2

Instagram account is Gabrielle Spierer

LinkedIn account is Gabrielle Spierer
http://www.linkedin.com/in/gabrielle-spierer-8b6180129

A Survivor's Story of Healing

Hi everyone. My name is Gabrielle Spierer, or Gabby, as most of my friends call me. I was honored that Donna asked me to write a chapter for this book. We met serendipitously in April of 2018 at the Global Sisterhood Conference in Pittsburgh. We sat next to each other during one of the group presentations, started talking, and hit it off. I had told the group that I was a domesic violence survivor and she had told me about her book, 'The Reinvention of Me' that had just been published. I bought a copy, we exchanged phone numbers, emails, and stayed in touch. It's remarkable how certain people are drawn together, and as a fellow survivor I was very happy to meet her!

While I'm honored to be contributing a chapter for this book on domestic violence, I'm also terrified to be writing it! I've been going to counselling for about ten years, but it wasn't until I started going to separate domestic violence counselling in the spring of 2018, that I realized how much I've been through and how much I continue to go through. Sharing with the world all of the experiences and pain that I've gone through and continue to go through is a very scary feeling. It's hard to talk about the personal parts of my life and allow myself to feel vulnerable to an audience of people I don't know. Getting my feelings out and sharing my life's journey and experiences with you is part of my healing and hopefully, it'll help you in your lives as well.

As you will see I'm experiencing three really significant journeys in my life. One is becoming my authentic self. The second is healing from the emotional and physical abuse I've experienced since I was a child, practically since I was born. The third is changing my laws of attraction to have healthier relationships. While my journey to authenticity is a lot in itself, I know the more difficult part of my life's journey is healing from the lifetime of abuse and working to have healthier relationships.

Sharing my journey to become my authentic self with everyone means revealing my former life. At some point, I'll share with you what that is. I've been told that part of my story is apparently a bit much for people and a little hard to hear and understand so I'm going to try to tell it in an easy way. I've always thought of it as a strength and something to be proud of that I use to try to help promote acceptance and understanding, but not everyone sees it that way. Many people call me courageous, and a role model. However, because of all of the bullying, discrimination, and subconscious biases I've experienced as well as my deep-seated abandonment issues, I still get triggered by emotionally abusive people. Consequently, I don't always feel very brave or heroic. I'm scared to put that part of my life out there to the world, but to overcome everything and move forward, I need to share all of it.

Healing from a lifetime of emotional and physical abuse as a child and emotional abuse as an adult,

71

especially in my second marriage of almost thirty years, has negatively affected my self-esteem and my sense of self. Even though my ex and I have been apart since mid-2013, and divorced since May 2016, I seemed to be repeating a pattern of being attracted to the same kind of narcissistic, emotionally abusive people. I'm always left with the feeling that I'm not respected, listened to, or treated with the kindness a person deserves!

It's amazing how the laws of attraction work subconsciously, and we're drawn to certain types of people influenced by our past. Sometimes they have similar personalities and at other times opposites are attracted to each other. It's regrettable when relationships are not very healthy. Perpetuating cycles based on the environments we were brought up in, and comfortable with, seems to be something we all do on some level whether we realize it or not. Breaking my cycle to have healthier relationships is something I'm aspiring to and working hard to achieve one day at a time!

I really began to realize this pattern when the relationship I was having with a close friend with whom I was sharing a house, started to go terribly wrong in the spring of 2018. You see, we had been friends for about ten years, and she and her mother, were like family to me. I really needed family and people to be close to after I moved out of the house my ex and I had shared since 1999.

Now, let's start at the beginning. You see, my story is a lot different than most people's experiences and life journey.

By all accounts, my family would be considered an American immigrant success story. All of my family, including my parents and grandparents, are from Hungary. My father was born in 1930 and my mother in 1935. My family is Jewish and lived through the horrors of two world wars, oppression, and anti-Semitism from the Hungarian government after WWI, the rise of the Nazis in the 1930s, the Holocaust, and the communists after WWII.

As you can imagine, what they experienced was horrific and the resulting trauma and PTSD affected them tremendously. It was a horrible time in the world. It wasn't until the 1980s that people began to understand the effects of PTSD. The anger, hypervigilance, emotional withdrawal, the need to control everything and everyone along with the associated abuse that many victims took out on their families.

My parents escaped during the Hungarian revolution in the fall of 1956 and with the help of the Hebrew Immigrant Aid Society (HIAS) settled in New York City. I was conceived in Hungary and born in America in April 1957. My sister was born three years later.

My mother took out all of her anger on both of us. We were terrified of her. When we were young, that statement that 'kids should be seen and not heard' was never more prevalent than in my family. If I

73

dared to challenge anything she said or did, I would be given that look where you feel like you want to die 1,000 times. I was never allowed to speak up, and if we questioned or disobeyed anything my mother told us to do, I would get beaten with the buckle end of a belt. Countless times I kneeled facing the corner of my room on a bare floor for hours just for questioning why I had to do something, or if I didn't get a grade of 100 on a test in school. My sister was the good girl and, to avoid all of the physical abuse, she just did as she was told. You see, we both had to be perfect, but then we were also told we were never good enough. It's an impossible task since no one's perfect!

Since we were an immigrant family and I was born shortly after my family arrived in the US, I didn't learn to speak English until I went to school. My mother had a very traditional way of thinking and made most of our clothes in the traditional European Hungarian/German style. It was very different from the way that kids in my neighborhood dressed. American kids dressed mostly in sneakers and jeans, while my mother felt that I should wear dress pants and a collared shirt. She never listened to my desire to blend in, and since I was dressed differently than most kids, I got bullied a lot in school.

My father, on the other hand, was withdrawn and never interacted with us. He just worked and watched TV. It was almost as if he didn't exist. My father worked hard in the restaurant business and made pretty good money, but it still wasn't good enough for my mother. We were doing all kinds of extra-curricular activities and she tried to push my father to work harder and make more money. He tried driving a taxicab but was uncomfortable with it and quit after one day. Instead of being compassionate and understanding about his difficulties, she berated him. I could never talk to my father about anything going on in his life or mine and we were never close. He definitely never shared any of what he went through in Europe.

All of the trauma and resulting PTSD he went through earlier in his life affected him so much that he wasn't emotionally strong enough to stand up to the bullying and verbal abuse from my mother, so he just withdrew. I think he gave up on dealing with my mother and they got divorced while I was in high school. I couldn't connect with either of my parents and I never felt like I was loved and accepted by either of them.

I said before that I'd talk about my journey to authenticity. I'm now going to tell you about it. At about the age of 10 years old, while my sister and I were going through all of these family difficulties, I found I had this need to dress in the clothes of the opposite sex. I used to go down to the basement of the Jewish temple we belonged to try on the women's clothes they sold at the rummage or garage sales. I also had no idea why I had the compulsion to do this. Since my mother was so unsympathetic and controlling, I could never tell her or anyone how I felt or what I was doing.

The world was a very different place in the 1960s, 70s, 80s, and even the 1990s! Remember, there were no cell phones, computers, or the internet. There was nothing in mainstream books, movies, or on TV. There was only some he/she videos and magazines in the adult sections of video stores in the 1990s. I vaguely remember hearing about Christine Jorgensen and Dr. Renee Richards, two pioneering transgender women in the 1960s and 70s, but it never registered with me that I was like them. Even if I had understood who I am at that time, if you said anything to anyone, they would think you were crazy, and you could be committed. I had NO ONE to talk to or who would listen to me, so I kept my feelings to myself.

Do you know the movie Mommy Dearest? Well, that's what it seemed to be like in my family. If you were on the outside looking in we looked like the perfect family. My parents worked hard, and we had a typical middle-class life. We got all of the material things that children could want. My mother put us in all sorts of activities like tap and modern dance, gymnastics, guitar, and piano lessons. On weekends we would go to museums or the Lincoln Center to see Leonard Bernstein's young children's concerts. While we got all of these material things, I had this tremendously empty feeling inside and I never truly felt like I was ever loved or accepted by either parent. This had nothing to do with my gender identity conflict. On top of that, whenever anyone discovered my alternate gender expression, my friendships or relationships ended so I had significant abandonment issues.

When we're born, we have this empty bucket that our parents are supposed to help us fill with unconditional love to help us grow. I didn't have that experience as a child because they were so traumatized that they emotionally withdrew and weren't able to have emotional connections or show love and affection. Most kids feel some love from both of their parents and some only feel it from one parent, but I didn't feel it from either parent! It's something I'm having to learn to do for myself and it's a very difficult and painful thing to do, but I know that it's the most important part of my journey so I can break the generational effects of the trauma and abuse.

My first marriage ended after five years in the early 1980s when my wife found out about my need to dress as a woman and express a different gender identity. I had this same feeling from my partners and friends who abandoned me when they found out that I wasn't a typical guy. I never had a supportive environment so I could safely express who I am and be myself. I always felt so abandoned and alone.

My second wife came from Central America where her family lived a very privileged life. Although she was privileged, my wife had a very difficult family life. Her mother, who was estranged from her own mother and raised by her maternal grandmother, was very abusive and emotionally withdrawn from my wife, her two brothers, and one sister. My spouse grew up in a very religious, traditional, and patriarchal environment. In the mid-1980s the family had to leave the country due to the civil war and immigrated to the US. It was a very traumatic time for my wife and her family. We met on Long Island through a personal ad in the late 1980s and got married in 1989. In the early 1990s, she found out about the other part of me and couldn't deal with it. She wasn't accepting of my alternate gender expression and instead of asking for a divorce, she became verbally and very emotionally abusive to me in an almost imperceptible way. The putdowns and the comments were so subtle that I didn't realize I was being verbally abused and manipulated. I so wanted to be loved that I even went through conversion therapy which was incorporated into the counselling I was already receiving.

I was so traumatized and used to a hurtful, negative, controlling environment, I didn't realize it was unacceptable to be treated that way and it seemed normal to me. What was worse, my wife never listened to anything that I had to say. We were never a couple or a team. When they say that you marry your parents, in our case it was absolutely true! We both were 'her' parents and we were 'my' parents. When you're not heard, acknowledged, or respected, it seriously affects your self-esteem. It was not a very healthy way to be. My wife felt what I was going through was just a phase and we had a son in 1992. I love my son and he's a blessing, but unfortunately, he grew up in this very emotionally dysfunctional environment. My wife and I were very separate, and in order to cope with things, I withdrew just like my father did. What little self-esteem I had was gone and I basically just worked and slept he had.

I had always been at the top of my class in school. Having attended Brooklyn Technical High School and Case Western Reserve University, I was able to get a good job and work as a mechanical design engineer. That changed in the early 1990s when the defense industry started to leave Long Island, New York. Consequently, I got a job working as an independent contractor for Newsday. It was early mornings, my own business, and I earned as much as I had earned as an engineer. Although I tried to suppress my feelings, my gender identity issues never went away, and it was always that unspoken elephant in the room. Since we worked opposite schedules, I always tried to express my true gender identity discreetly when my wife and my son weren't home. It didn't prove to be enough and I was still very unhappy. I knew that all of the emotional abuse and lack of opportunity to be true to myself was taking a significant physical and psychological toll on my mind and body.

In the early 2000s with the greater access to information from the internet, I began to realize that there were many more people like me, and I wasn't the only one. I was slowly dying one day at a time, but then when my mother passed on December 7th, 2007, I knew I had to be truer to myself. Her repressive presence was gone. That led to my new growth and realization that I was really a transgender woman and born into the wrong body. When I was conceived, my body was born one way and my mind was born another. In my case, my mind was born female and my body was born male. In order to be my authentic self, I had to make my mind and body match.

Our gender is the most important aspect of who we are. Whether you're male, female, or somewhere in between, it's our most fundamental core identity. We have other identities relating to our ethnicity, religion, profession, race, being a parent, single, part of a couple, or family, but our gender is our core. Most people don't think about their gender. It just comes naturally and so subconsciously to them. Who they are feels right and they just go about their lives without giving it a second thought. Since gender is our core identity, when you're rejected for who you are, it hurts tremendously and it's the most painful experience you can have as a transgender individual. In my case, I had to go through a lot of pain and deep soul searching to realize and understand who I am. I have to say it's the most wonderful feeling to be able to have your mind and body match.

So much has changed since mid-2013 now that I'm fully living as my authentic self. I've completely changed my life. After working every day except Christmas at Newsday for 23 years, I was tired, so I went back to school full time to get my social work Degree in Counselling. I wanted to do something meaningful with the rest of my life. In addition to understanding gender, I've gained a tremendous understanding of trauma, abuse, bullying, domestic violence, and its effects. Therefore, I want to help people who need to work through those issues. I've spoken at colleges, high schools, and other venues about gender, being your authentic self, and having accepting people in your life who can support whatever your journey in life is.

I've given workshops at conferences on *Strategies for Successfully Coming Out at Work* both individually and as a panel discussion. I've also done workshops on *The Power of Authenticity, Making Change and Its Effects on the World Around Us*, *Having Supportive People in Our Lives When We Make Change* and *The Importance of Having A Family of Choice*. In 2019 I gave a speech at the Suffolk County Long Island, New York Commemoration Day Event, which honors domestic violence survivors, and emphasizes their struggles during October's Domestic Violence Awareness Month. In 2019 they highlighted stories of healing from survivors regardless of their sexual orientation, gender expression, or gender identity.

Writing a chapter for this book with nine other authors and survivors of domestic violence has also been cathartic and is helping me in my healing.

At the same time, I've continued going to counselling. In addition to my regular counselling, since the spring of 2018, I've added EMDR (Eye Movement Rapid Desensitization) counselling. It's a proven experiential method of counselling I learned about it from a class I took in school. It was originally used to help treat combat veterans experiencing PTSD or Post Traumatic Stress Disorder. It's now used for many types of trauma patients and helps heal the traumatized part of our brains. The EMDR process helps to reroute the brain waves around the traumatized area of our mind so we can heal from traumatic events.

Additionally, after my experience where I was living, when I realized that my environment was very emotionally abusive, I also added domestic violence counselling. Combining all of these types of counselling, especially the EMDR therapy is helping me to heal my mind and feel more whole than I've ever felt before! My memory is significantly better and coming back, especially the blocked ones. Feelings of anger, and anxiety, as well as compulsions and self-defeating behaviors have also diminished. I'm learning to love myself to fill that empty bucket and forgive the people from my past. I'm also putting more supportive, accepting people into my life, and working on changing the types of people that I'm attracted to. Everyone deserves to be treated with respect and kindness.

Since all my life I've been so starved for love and acceptance when anyone showed me a little kindness, I easily let them into my life. Many times, they weren't healthy for me. Now when I meet people, I take more time to get to know them before I emotionally let them into my life.

Yes, I'm doing all of this to heal so I can overcome a lifetime of abuse and have a much happier life going forward, but the most important reason I'm going through all of this pain is really for the love of my child. He grew up in a very dysfunctional house, and with all of the issues, he never got the love and emotional support that every child needs to grow up in an emotionally healthy way. After we separated, I thought that if my ex and I could be friends, it would help us to heal and show our son that we can be more of a team which would help him to heal. It was difficult and I knew I was putting myself back into a very unhealthy situation, but I felt that I needed to try so I could build a better relationship with my son. Standing up to my abuser was also helping me take my power back.

Every one of us that goes through any form of life change or transition has to look inside ourselves so we can try to understand who we are. Working through my gender issues helped me realize that I had lived through a lifetime of bullying, emotional and physical abuse as a child, and extreme emotional abuse as an adult, especially during my marital relationship of 25 years. The trauma and resulting PTSD I experienced severely affected my self-esteem and I was repeating the same unhealthy patterns in my relationships. So, while going through my gender transition is significant enough for almost anyone, the more significant and difficult part of my journey has been the healing from the lifetime of domestic violence I've experienced! I always say that being transgender saved my emotional life since I had to look at my entire life and all of my relationships. Being a member of one of the most maligned, discriminated, and misunderstood minority groups saved my life. I'm proud and honored to be part of a community of some of the bravest and most amazing people in the world!

In closing, everything that I've gone through has severely impacted my life in an unhealthy way. By going through all of this counselling, introspection and emotional pain, my goal is to break the cycle of the transferred generational effects of the trauma, heal from everything I've been through, and be aware of my attractions. Hopefully, this will help me go from having unhealthy relationships to healthier ones. Most importantly, I also would like to be have a better connection with my son so he can truly feel loved and have a significantly healthier emotional life, at a much earlier age, than I did. To me, helping my son help himself is the most important part of my journey. If there's anything that I succeed at doing during my life, building a better relationship with my son would be it. Like I said before, I'm going through all of this for the love of my child and to continue overcoming the effects of my past relationships to build a healthier ones. Making change isn't easy, but we can all do it one day at a time!

Covid-19 and the Effects of

Social Isolation

Shortly after the beginning of the Covid-19 lockdown my friend walked into a room to ask her partner a question and was yelled and cursed at for no apparent reason by him. She was quite astonished and upset at the abusive behavior she experienced. Later on, when she tried to talk to him about it, he never apologized and wasn't remorseful, so nothing was resolved. She told me that she felt very belittled and verbally abused.

A week later it happened again. This time they went shopping at the supermarket. My friend told me they went early in the morning before work to avoid the crowds. They were in line at the checkout when she realized they forgot something and went to go get it. By the time she returned her partner had already checked out and was waiting very impatiently to leave. My friend said she was yelled at in front of everybody for not getting back fast enough. Later on, she tried to talk to her partner after she cooled down, but nothing was ever settled, and he never thought his behavior was inappropriate. My friend was very upset about what happened and was crying as she told me the story. She also said that although there were signs about his behavior, he had never yelled, cursed at her, or reacted that way in stressful situations. I tried to reassure her that things will get better as we adapt to the stress created from going into lockdown and we figure out how to work from home.

I know things have been very different since the coronavirus lockdown started. Nerves are frazzled, and tempers are shorter. Working entire days from home during isolation is very different from working in an office during the day and taking extra work home nights and weekends even if you're used to sitting at a computer all day.

The totally disruptive way that the coronavirus affected our lives came as a shock to almost everyone. It came swiftly and spread like wildfire through Asia, Europe and then to the US. Within the span of a few weeks we went into lockdown. All of our lives have been turned completely upside down. It created a very difficult time of uncertainty and increased everyone's level of anxiety. Millions of people lost their jobs, and many started having difficulties paying their bills and or even have enough money to buy food for their families. According to the New York Times the pandemic has caused a significant increase in the number of calls to domestic violence organizations from people around the world. In one way or another everyone's lives have been changed forever.

In another New York Times article entitled 'For Abused Women, a Pandemic Lockdown Holds Dangers of its Own', one survivor, Maggie, 25, who's working on healing from an abusive relationship she left five years ago, said that in recent weeks, her weekly therapy appointment has moved online and her support group was cancelled altogether, which has made it even more difficult for her to cope with her increased isolation. As a result, she said she has fallen back into unhealthy coping mechanisms, like drinking and smoking.

"I imagine many survivors, even if they are safe in their home, are experiencing long hours of sitting alone with traumatic thoughts and nightmares due to increased anxiety," Maggie said.

After hearing my friend's stories and reading these articles, I started thinking what if that happened to me? How would I feel and react? What would I do if my partner, close friend, or family member did that to me? How would I try to stay positive when I've been through so much negativity?

Even before the pandemic I was doing some self-isolating so I could focus on healing from everything I've been through and deal with all of the loss I had experienced. I used the time for introspection, to be kind to myself and to work on putting more positive people into my life through virtual social gatherings so I could maintain a more positive outlook. I know that language is important, and I started to pay attention to what I was hearing. I was determined to build up my inner strength and change the negative voices in my head that I've been hearing since I've been born.

Before Covid-19 I had difficulties whenever I had to deal with my ex and many times with my son as well. During the pandemic it is easier for them to ghost me or avoid talking to me since I physically couldn't go and visit them. I had to allow myself to be hurt and upset over what was happening and look at the big picture. I love my son, so all I could is to keep setting an example and understand that everything happens in its own time and in its own way. I can only do my part and as an adult he has to do his, otherwise our relationship will never work. I realized that no matter how I approach things with my ex, she and I were not going to be able to be friends and eventually I will be able to remove the negativity from my life.

I watched heartwarming shows or movies and focused on the positive aspects of the character's relationships. Every day I wrote a gratitude list of 5 things. I told a friend to say something positive about me every day and I told her that I would the same for her. By focusing on something more positive I was able to reduce my level of anxiety about what was happening and be able to keep seeing things in a more positive way.

I always try to see myself as a survivor and not a victim. Emotional pain isn't easy to deal with, but I kept telling myself that the pain is part of self-care and I'm healing my old wounds to make new more positive thoughts and change the voices in my head.

Every one of us can start by taking one small positive step and then keep adding to it a little bit at a time. You should also take time to enjoy the journey and one day when you look back, you'll realize that you're come a long way and are a lot further ahead than you thought.

At the end of my chapter called *'A Survivor's Story of Healing'*, I said that healing from difficult relationships and making changes to your life takes a concerted effort. The path from point A to point B is never a straight line and at times it's okay to tread water, go sideways, and even go backwards for a while. We ALL deserve kindness, respect, and good people in our lives. What's most important is to always be kind to yourself and know that tomorrow is another day where you can start fresh and chart a new course to move forward making change one day at a time!

Chapter 5

Gem Rose

Accidentally falling into her dream career as a performer in her late teens, Gem has spent the last two decades performing around the world to audiences of thousands, garnering acclaim from famous fans such as Professor Stephen Hawking, and sharing her gifts with students of all ages. Through her performing arts school, adult choir, online and offline courses, blogs, and podcasts, Gem inspires people to find their voice, express their creativity, grow in confidence, and become part of a community. Now happily married, Gem lives by the sea, competing in Triathlons, mountain biking, hiking, and eating copious amounts of vegan cake.

www.gemrose.me
www.facebook.com/gemroseuk
www.arosebetweenthornsblog.blogspot.com

Freedom

I was warned about him. I was warned that he was a liar and a cheat, and a nightmare with women. I believed it at first, told him to stay away, I was seeing somebody else anyway. But he made me feel like I was the most incredible, beautiful, talented, fascinating goddess that had ever lived, and that we were destined to be together. So, when the guy I had been seeing cheated, I fell into Paul's arms. (Not his real name.)

We were so in love, so perfect for each other, we liked all the same things, wanted the same life together. "Ha"! I thought, "we've proven you all wrong; we're the perfect couple, and Paul is the perfect partner". But I had never heard of the terms *narcissistic abuse* or *love bombing* as I was clueless as to what was about to happen.

For the first few months, Paul showered me with attention, affection, compliments, gifts, his time. I had finally found the one. And then about eight months in, I found out he'd been making plans behind my back to go away on a trip and had been lying about it for weeks. I was upset and annoyed that he had been lying to me. We'd both agreed from the start that we needed total and utter honesty from each other to make the relationship work, and he had convinced me that we were on the same page.

He spent three days apologising and crying, begging forgiveness, he'd never lie again, etc. etc. So we moved on, but that had broken the seal. I had seen behind his mask, and that made him angry.

The next incident I remember, it was as though someone had flipped a switch in him. We were at his parents' house. I don't even remember what had happened, but he went crazy, screaming and shouting in my face, his face pink and swollen, veins bulging out of his skin, his eyes full of hatred at me. I'd never seen him like this and it was terrifying. I began to cry but he kept screaming, angry eyes piercing into me while I stood frozen to the spot with fear, and then eventually he stormed downstairs, slammed the front door, and screeched away in his car.

I stood there for a while, quivering and crying, and then I heard his Dad calling upstairs to me, "Gemma ...come here love." I slowly ambled down the stairs, still crying and shaking, and his Dad shook his head sadly. "He was just like this with the last one," he said. Paul had told me that his last girlfriend was a psycho, jealous, controlling, etc., and I'd believed him, but seeing his father's face at that moment, I began to doubt that.

Not long after, Paul and I moved in together and had a lovely Christmas in our new home. But only a few days into January things went sour again. I'd suspected him of contacting other women behind my back, so when he went out one day I checked his phone, and my suspicions were confirmed. On his return, I gave him a chance to be honest about it, which of course he wasn't, and when I told him I had seen his phone he flew into a rage. He smashed up the apartment, screamed that she was just a friend, I was paranoid, I was a psycho, and it was my fault he had to sneak around because I was so jealous and controlling, just like his ex.

There's a tendency in society to very easily label women with the 'psycho girlfriend' stereotype if they raise completely legitimate objections to unreasonable behaviour from a partner. It's a type of gaslighting, to make the other person believe that they are the one being unreasonable, and I got swept up in this. I didn't want to be *that woman* and so I changed my behaviour, instead of Paul changing his.

The psychotic rages came thick and fast after that though, and the catalysts for them became stranger. One winter evening we went to a music shop so I could buy a tambourine, but I wasn't sure I wanted the one he thought I should get, so he became angry. He started growling at me under his breath and I could see people looking at us, so I tried to calmly suggest we had to think about it and come back another day. "NO", Paul said, "WE'RE GETTING ONE NOW". The store manager was watching us now and I just wanted out, so again I tried to calmly shrug it off and say we would come back another time. "NO. WE CAME HERE TO GET A F**KING TAMBOURINE, SO WE'RE GETTING A F**KING TAMBOURINE".

I walked out of the shop and he came screaming after me, calling me names, and ranting. He ordered me back into the shop and when I didn't go he jumped in his car, swerved it round in front of me, and barked at me to get in, which I did, and he then began to speed erratically out of the car park. He realised he'd turned the wrong way, threw the car into reverse, and backed straight into the side of another car. "NOW LOOK WHAT YOU'VE MADE ME DO YOU F**KING BITCH!!".

I was scared and anxious and I just wanted to be away from him. It was dark and cold but while he was talking to the driver of the other car I saw my chance to slip away and began walking down the road. He obviously realised shortly after that I had gone and ran after me, abandoning his car in the road, yelling expletives and insults as he chased me, but I'd had a fair head start so I just kept running until I couldn't hear him anymore.

I slowed down and kept walking, legs like jelly, silently crying until I heard him again, he'd gone back to retrieve the car and was now shouting furiously out of the car window, holding up the other traffic behind him. "GET IN THE F**KING CAR!!!" I sobbed sadly for him to please just leave me alone. He yelled a few more times, the cars behind him now beeping for him to speed up and get out of the way, and I just kept walking, head down, tears rolling down my face. Eventually, he gave one last expletive out of the window and zoomed off. I walked for over an hour to home on my own in the dark and the cold, scared but so relieved to be away from him.

I couldn't believe we'd had a crazy scene like that over a tambourine. That wasn't me being jealous or possessive, but it was somehow still my fault? I remember so many incidents like that, but I don't remember how most of them started, which shows how little it took to set him off; the tiniest, minutest perceived criticisms, the slightest thing not going the way he wanted it to.

I was terrified of him. So why didn't I leave? Because for every crazy outburst of rage, there were a dozen adorable, sweet, affectionate outpourings of love. I had still never heard of narcissistic abuse, and I believed that my poor, loving, caring boyfriend simply had an anger problem, and needed help. I somehow managed to drag him along to an assessment with a relationship counsellor who spoke with us for an hour and confirmed what I'd thought, that we did not need couples therapy, that the issue was with Paul, but Paul would not take the advice of a trained professional. As far as he was concerned, he did not have a problem. Very occasionally, he would have a moment of weakness, or clarity, or maybe just pure manipulation, and agree that he needed help and would seek it, but that was always forgotten the next day.

I tried speaking to his parents and his friends, but by this point, he'd done such a good job of convincing them all that I was the crazy one that they were no help. Paul was a prolific liar, pathologically so. Even when he had been caught red-handed in a lie he would still keep lying. It was unnerving to see, and he once admitted to me that he lied so deeply that he would make himself almost believe his own lies. So most of his friends came to hate me. They were not nice people, and Paul would let them treat me appallingly. He would prioritise everybody above me, I was at the bottom of the list, always. He would purposefully humiliate me in front of them, physically push me around, and scream at me in their presence. They didn't care, they thought it was funny.

One time I called Paul from work to say I'd forgotten my house keys. He said he'd be home when I got back but he wasn't, so I called round to his parents, and when I went in, he was sitting in their lounge with another girl. He smiled at me smugly. I asked him for his keys so I could leave but he said no, he wanted me to stay and chat with him and his *friend*, and when I refused he flipped again, grabbed me, pushed me out of the room, along the hall, out the front door, and then threw my shoes at me. He later admitted that he had set it up on purpose so that I would have to go to his parents and find him there with her.

Narcissistic abuse isn't all beatings and yelling, it's little things like that, playing with your mind, little things but they all add up, and they are done to purposefully demoralise you and break your spirit, making sure you never feel settled and at peace. Constantly keeping you in a state of limbo so that they have utter control over both your happiness or your despair. He had me convinced that I was lucky to have him and that nobody else would ever want me.

I had been a happy person before him. I had a job I enjoyed, I lived in a lovely apartment with friends. I had a wide social circle, I was fit and healthy and mentally strong. He robbed me of all of that. Over the four years we were together, he entirely destroyed me. Years of living on the edge of my nerves, wondering what would set him off next, spending my life just trying to please him, having my

96

possessions smashed / thrown / ripped apart, finding his secret social media profiles, messages from other women, his obsessive porn addiction, spending nights sleeping on the bathroom floor because he was locked on the other side of the door growling and threatening me. Or spending nights not sleeping at all because he'd disappeared again and wouldn't answer the phone, being dragged out of a car by my ankle, humiliated in public, called every name under the sun.

I lost my friends and quit my job. My confidence withered away and I stopped having contact with anyone because I was too ashamed for them to know what my life had become. I stopped eating, stopped sleeping, stopped leaving the house. I became painfully thin, completely isolated, and more depressed than I knew was possible.

It came to a head one evening. He had temporarily moved back in with his parents and I was home alone in a dark, damp, moldy apartment. I had lost everything, externally and internally. I wasn't me anymore, I was just a frail, exhausted body, with no hope of ever being happy or living a normal life again, and I couldn't take the pain anymore. I needed out. I called him, he didn't answer. I sent him a message, begged him to come over and sit with me for a while. I couldn't remember the last time I'd seen another person, he was all I had, I just needed another human presence for a while. I told him I couldn't cope any longer, I was in too much pain, I couldn't go on living. He told me he couldn't come over because he and Vicky (not her real name) had just ordered a pizza.

I scoured the house for old packets of sleeping pills, Paracetamol, Ibuprofen, and took whatever I could find, I just needed to not be alive. I don't know when I woke up, but I woke up. I was still alive. And I took him back again.

Until recently, I have mostly felt the after-effects of the mental and emotional abuse more than the physical, the giving and then withholding of love, the blatant disrespect, disappearing with no contact, the gaslighting, convincing me that I was utterly worthless and undeserving of love, the name-calling, etc. But a few weeks ago I was watching something on TV and there was a scene featuring the stereotypical couple who have it all, walking home from a party together and going in their front door, when all of a sudden the man turned and punched his wife in the stomach. I felt as though I had been punched in the stomach.

There it was, that old, almost forgotten, feeling of suddenly being attacked. Suddenly being grabbed by the throat, or picked up and thrown across the room, or suddenly having a contorted, twisted, enraged face pressed up against mine, screaming abuse before head butting me. It all came flooding back. I felt as though I couldn't breathe, my heart was racing and I began to cry. I had almost forgotten that feeling. That fear. The fear of wondering if this time was going to be the time he eventually went too far and did actually kill me. He threatened several times.

Once when I questioned him about going away for two days with no contact he told me that if I didn't stop talking he would punch me in the face until I died and bury my body in the back garden – and at that moment I absolutely believed that this man who'd once convinced me I was the most wonderful person he'd ever met, really was capable of putting his fist through my face until I stopped breathing.

It's terrifying to know that I was so completely fooled by someone, that I allowed someone so much control and power over me. It seems melodramatic to call what I'm left with now PTSD, but the symptoms are there, a scene on TV, a song, a place, someone's behaviour, it all brings back horrific memories and induces fear, crying, sickness, etc. But at least I got out, I am one of the lucky ones.

It was Paul who initially ended the relationship. He told me months later that he never actually intended us to split and that he'd left temporarily to emotionally bribe me into changing my ways (letting him do whatever he wanted), but it backfired on him enormously. At first, I was broken. I couldn't sleep or eat again, I cried constantly, but this time instead of withdrawing into myself, I fought to keep my head above water. I knew I could not bear to sink as low as I had before. So, I called friends, I let them comfort me, I forced myself to eat a little, then a little more. I forced myself to get out of the house, to attempt some exercise, to see other humans and socialise. And when he came back a few weeks later, I no longer wanted him. I was free.

I am now in the healthiest relationship of my life. It is, quite honestly, blissful. My husband gives me more affection, attention, and love than I need – and not the on / off, conditional kind of love of a narcissistic abuser. He does not give love that he thinks I should be grateful for (although I am), he gives the pure, warts-and-all kind of love that is ALWAYS there, even if I'm being unreasonable, or he's in a bad mood, or something didn't go his way that day. Yes, I still have the hangover from Paul, never quite believing I'm enough, struggling most days to understand what my wonderful husband could possibly see in me, constantly worrying that his mood is entirely dependent on me and that it is my job to make sure he is always having / doing / being exactly what he wants, endlessly trying not to be the controlling partner Paul convinced everyone (and almost me) that I was. But I am feeling the fear and doing it anyway. I will not let a mixed-up man from my past ruin the chance of a lifetime for my today and my tomorrow.

So, I fight every day to make myself believe that I am worthy of love. It is not my husband's job to constantly convince me of that (although he would if I asked him to), it is my job to trust in the love he shows me and work on my self-esteem until I see myself the way he does.

It's difficult to properly cover narcissistic abuse in one chapter. Unless you have experienced it, it is incredibly difficult to explain. We can comprehend stories of partners who fly into jealous rages and physically attack, that seems straightforward, but how do you explain a million tiny, minute manipulations.

If you are to take one thing from my chapter, I want it to be that IT DOES NOT HAVE TO BE LIKE THAT. Paul had me utterly convinced that he was my only option in life, but that is never the case. If you are with someone who abuses you, they are not the one. If you are with someone who makes you feel unloveable, you are being abused. If any of this seems familiar to you, I urge you to research the terms:

Narcissistic Abuse

Love Bombing

Gaslighting

Abuse is not just physical. Any kind of abuse is unacceptable. And any kind of abuse is survivable. There is life after abuse. I have found it, and I am loving it.

Chapter 6

Dr. Melisa

D r. Melisa. is an Integrative psychotherapist in the field of Mind-Body Medicine. A free spirit and highly committed individual who continues to transform and heal on her journey. She is here to bring healing to others and to teach the ways to live in harmony, from the heart, with ourselves, each other, and the more than human world! Heart Wide Open!!!

Lets go back in time. It was the end of summer days and this young, 20-year-old girl was attempting to drive her car away as a man grabbed her head with one hand and with the other held a tire iron. At that moment, outside that old farmhouse, she wondered if this would be the end of her life.

Her thoughts went to the woman who had lived in this same old farmhouse many years before, alone with 20 cats, she wondered if that woman had found the answer. This girl who felt like she never belonged, never seemed to do the right thing, and now her so-called husband was threatening to bash her head in. Well, yes she did survive and that 20-year-old girl is now this 52-year-old woman. Here is my story.

Let's start with my background. Abuse, domestic violence, had been a huge part of my life. I would never know a *normal.* I learned to live and by the way, very functionally, in this trauma-filled life. How did I live so functionally well? That would be the so-called gift of adaptation and disassociation. Now, I never knew I was disassociated throughout my life. I just seemed to deal extremely well with all types of trauma, at least in the moment, yet the whole of my life would oscillate between bouts of suicidal depression, disassociation, ongoing emotional avoidance and overwhelm, hypervigilance, anxiety, and anger.

I have lived in trauma mode. This mode consisted of the flight, fight, or freeze response, with my first choice being flight and second fight. Furthermore, in this surreal existence, I had the added pressure of always presenting myself as NORMAL. I had to keep it together ... yes, and I did that normal thing well. With the disassociation and the rationalizations of the famous "yes but" ... it is not so bad ... but these parts are good, you know ... and on and on...

I always felt a very real pressure to present myself as having it all together throughout my life. Abuse, especially in childhood, teaches us to be normal in the most of dysfunctional situations. I learned that well. My most important reason for being normal or acting normal was that I wanted both of my children to have a much better life, a normal life. Therefore, I started counselling at the ripe age of 20 and began my psychology education with the goals to heal and be a great mother: to protect my children from addiction, trauma, and abuse. However, it didn't work out exactly as I had planned.

My children

My daughter was born to me at the very young age of 19. I knew I wasn't in a good place to have a baby, but I felt I had to do the right thing and raise her to the best of my ability. This daughter, this beautiful little baby of mine, when she was young, I struggled. I was a young mom, financially stressed, and trying to figure out why I was always wanting to exit this Earth. Throughout her life, I worked so diligently and daily to protect her from the abuse and neglect of my life, however, she walked the walk of trauma with me. The exact thing I worked so hard to protect her from. Life truly is ironic.

Now she never would experience the same types of trauma that I endured but yes, my healing would take time and the trauma that was so deeply ingrained in me would be a part of every decision and most actions in life. Her and my relationship was tumultuous: my overprotection and emotional sensitivity and her independent personality and rebellious nature, collided often. However, as I raised her, mostly on my own, I attained my Master's in Counselling and was able to work and provide for us. My goal was for her and I to be in a position to never depend on a man again. While raising her, I grew up with her. I made a lot of mistakes but also made many good decisions, I realize that now. I left her abusive father, chose to live alone for the next seven years so we could be more secure, and never allowed drugs and alcohol to be in our home. I also worked diligently on my healing by doing a lot of therapy, holistic healing, and psychology training.

Moving forward in my life. When I was 27 years old I met the man I would be with for the next 20 years. This man, he was a dichotomy of many things. He was honest, an alcoholic, sweet, sensitive, humble, and also a creative genius. We got pregnant, accidentally, when I was 28 years of age. We broke up shortly after because I refused to deal with his angry outbursts and his drugs and alcohol. However, we got back together the day I was induced to bring my son into this world.

This beautiful baby boy born to me would bring me a gift of healing. I felt a deep sense of belonging, love, and attachment to this little soul. It seemed like I could do everything right by him. I was so grateful

105

as I sat in the hospital and held him, that I had chosen to keep him with me, especially because my entire pregnancy had been haunted with an everyday heaviness of what was best for this child. Was I selfish to keep this baby, what if he could have a life with a functional family? From the time I was young when other girls would get excited about future prospects of marriage and babies, I always had this deep feeling that children were not a good idea for me due to the level of addiction and mental illness in my family. However, the gifts we receive; my heart was wide open.

Move forward now 16 years later, my life is completely falling apart - the counsellor, the teacher, the wisdom holder for others, and yet my reality is crashing all around me. There were so many things in my life that were good most of the time, but the other truth is what was hidden from my eyes, through disassociation. Dissociation, like magic, would make everything seem okay, it made the bad seem less bad and allowed me to focus on the good things in my life. So how did the disassociation begin? How is this life crashing all around me? Well, we must go back to see how the journey of abuse, neglect, and domestic violence began for me and how disassociation became such a part of my life.

Domestic Violence: My Little History

My childhood was filled with fear, trauma, abuse, and a family that did, and still do, completely deny, without any acknowledgement of the severe neglect, abuse, and trauma that I endured in my childhood.

Let's start here. I didn't have a secure attachment with either of my parents. My father was a creative, loving, alcoholic, and a quite aggressive man. After a lifetime of drug/alcohol addiction and mental health, he died a few years ago, by himself, living in the back of a grocery store, homeless, far from the days of being a NASA employee. My father was a free spirit and I would connect with him so deeply as a little girl but his addiction and aggression always made him unsafe. He was unpredictable, his moods would change quickly, and at times just pure crazy behavior. He would be drunk and leave my brother and I in many different sketchy situations.

Of course, I would try to take care of my brother and would feel responsible. Let's say hello to the fix-it co-dependent as she begins her journey. As I got older, he would scare me, at times he would be so messed up, he would think I was my mother. He also became more unstable as his addiction progressed and became verbally abusive and threatening at times. Sadly, my last conversation with my father on this Earth was verbally abusive. I was tired of the verbal abuse and his control and domination so my protector showed up and I cussed, yelled, and screamed with a stop just long enough to ask him how he liked it. I stood up to him that day and told him I would no longer tolerate his verbal abuse. I hung up on him and sat in the parking lot of the local theatre sobbing from my soul. Why does it have to be this way? I love him, is he okay, why does he do this, I absolutely can't deal with this.

My mother. I still don't know to this day why she ever kept me as a baby. She was so young, a mom just 16 years of age. She decided to keep my brother and I, and on her 17th birthday she would have a little boy, and there was only 11 months between us. We lived with my mom, until my 3rd birthday, then we were sent to live with my grandmother. We would live in this little town in the West Virginia mountains with family, love, and safety from the ages of 3 to 8. I would miss my Mom. I remember running in my Grandma's circular driveway after my Mom would leave because I would be upset. I would consider these to be the best years of growing up. I became a nature girl, with the trees, the wind, and the water. I would feel such a sense of safety and connection with nature and living with my grandparents.

Except for my uncle and a few cousins attempting to engage sexually with me, I was safe. My grandma, she was a role model for me. She was a caretaker and a community therapist (not titled or paid).

In my eighth year of life, I had no idea how much my life was going to change. I am about to meet the man who is going to abuse and terrify me for the next five years.

On a rainy night, my Grandmother drove me three and a half hours away to Virginia. I am told I have to move in with my Mom and her significant other, George. I remember that night so vividly. I could, in this moment, literally touch my Grandmother's face. I remember the rain on the window, crying and begging her to take me with her. She said, "I am sorry, Missy, there is nothing I can do". She will say this many times to me throughout my life. Just three days later, the beatings began. The first one was for crying about missing my Grandma. From this point on, the next five years for me are focused on my survival of this man.

This man over the next five years will beat me with a board, switches and belts. He will lock me in cellars, grab and drag me by my hair while beating me with a belt, and threaten me that if I tell anyone he will kill me. He will wake me up in the middle of the night to look at water drops on a glass and then beat me with a switch as I bend over the dining room chair. He will make me sleep in my bed that I wetted in from the night before. While this is going on, people in the community, my family, my Grandma are aware and do NOTHING. Even my aunt who worked at the local health department looked the other way. My Grandma said she couldn't help me. I begged her to hide me, to protect me, but she said she couldn't go against my mother. What does this say to that child? Survive it, make it okay, we can't have a voice, etc.

The end of my childhood abuse, five years later, happened in the summer between my 8th and 9th-grade school year. I snuck out with a boy. He wasn't a true love to me, he wasn't what I imagined would be my first love, but he was 18 and I was going to run away with him. He was my way out. Well, I got caught sneaking out and therefore the beatings began. I received somewhere around 10 to 13 beatings that night. He would continue to say I was lying and then would have me bend over, grab my ankles, and beat me again and again with the switch. I distinctly remember my mother towards the end, yelling upstairs, that is enough.

This is the last beating I will ever endure from this man. That is because the next day, at school, I bled through my jeans, and a whole series of events began which would mean I would never be abused by this man again. He was never charged, he was never held accountable, nor was my mother. She states she didn't know. She did. I never once in my life saw or witnessed my mother being abused, just her children.

And even in my 20's as I began therapy, I will never forget her words when I told her about therapy and the abuse and she said, "well Melisa, you instigated problems with him". Until this day she has never acknowledged and/or apologized for any of her part in the neglect and/or abuse to me.

Let's move forward in time to where I came crashing into reality. Even though I had been in therapy since I was a young woman, now in my late 40's, I realized as I sat in my trauma therapist's office, that to survive my life, to survive the abuse, to create a normal life, I had lived a disassociated life.

The therapist was telling my husband and I that we needed to separate due to domestic violence. I was in shock, this was about my son's addiction, my trauma, and yes, we have some problems, but really, domestic violence? We are best friends, or are we? He doesn't control where I go or what I do, he supports me completely, right? However, reality was distorted.

Sitting here in her office my disassociated life disintegrated right before my eyes. In this relationship, what was also true, is that the majority of issues I blamed and gave myself responsibility and fault. I would tell myself that if I would just do more therapy, talk sweeter, be less demanding, less critical and more understanding so things would work better.

I would rationalize the parts of our relationship that were abusive. The anger, the screaming, the shutting down of communication, the threatening, and the straight-out name-calling, and verbal abuse. The fights that happened after my son would go to bed where I was told I was a 'f****** bitch', 'f****** whore', and 'why didn't I go and f*** myself'. Of course, my predominant worry was that this would wake up our son. I am sure he was awake, now, but at the time I truly thought maybe he didn't hear, the gift of disassociation. I justified the arguments, the throwing or hitting items around, especially if I would accidentally get hit by something flying in the air.

After many years of healing, trauma and crisis, my anger, my protection, my rage could not tolerate this anymore. I would not back down. I was like a wolf that had been attacked and beaten down and in our final argument I was attacking/protecting back. Just like my final conversation with my Dad so many years ago.

Here is what happened, through my deep trauma work. I stopped being a pleaser, making everything my fault, expecting anyone to validate me, and was able to see the reality of my son's addiction, my co-dependency, and my marriage. I started having healthy boundaries, deciding I have a right to peace and love in my life and my 20-year relationship ended.

So today, forward four years, it is now October of 2019 and I am sitting on a plane, with a guy who doesn't scare me ever, typing MY story. What I want to say to you after all of this is that now my "life is all sunshine and daydreams." However, here is my truth. I am learning about real love, how to grow in love, to trust, to be me without cutting off parts to please others (so hard), and how to speak my true voice.

I am learning that each person has their story, but that they also have responsibility for their actions, and I don't rationalize and make the unacceptable acceptable or take responsibility that is not mine. I also take responsibility for my issues and problems. I don't, nor will I, tolerate verbal abuse anymore.

I am working on my co-dependent addiction at a much deeper level and will be as I continue to grow on my healing journey.

I understand now that healing is messy but, day-by-day, I am getting there. I do live in peace now. I am in a safe place but I am still working at bringing that peacefulness inside of me. I now invite all of the parts of me into my life. I spend much time in nature for healing, and I continue doing my healing work with others.

Final Notes:

The domestic violence pattern begins with so many as children. We see and experience trauma. We are not protected or validated by the people who are to love and protect us. We suffer low self-esteem. We don't feel secure attachment.

Domestic violence changes when we heal, when we develop self-respect and boundaries, and when we learn that loving others doesn't mean accepting abuse from them or us.   When we learn that forgiving doesn't mean to continue being in someone's life who is unwilling to heal and/or grow or abuse us.

Domestic violence doesn't look the same for all people, what if we don't term people good or bad, but we acknowledge the cycle, the pattern, whether the relationship is good 70% percent of the time; abuse of any kind isn't okay and that requires boundaries and honesty with ourselves and others.

To heal, use whatever guides your soul, but I highly recommend trauma therapy such as EMDR or body-based therapies that help heal the past trauma and integrate all the parts that have disassociated due to trauma.

We all need to heal, to change, to grow, and find our way. This is what changes the world. Love to each of you on this journey. Hearts Wide Open!!

Chapter 7

Alicia Sanchez

My goal is to have different avenues to help empower women and bring global awareness about the challenges we face. You can follow my journey on Facebook at Angelical Healing Hearts Home and IG @ Angelical Healing Hearts Miniseries.

My Journey

A personal encounter

As a survivor of abusive relationships, having faced the challenges of being a teen mom, I am now a passionate advocate trying to educate and raise awareness about domestic violence, in hopes of one day opening transitional housing for young women suffering from Domestic Violence. Through my real estate experience, I acquired a property that I am currently remodeling for my Ministry. Angelical Healing Hearts Home Ministry will offer transitional housing for young women.

This chapter has been very difficult to write, as you will see my encounter with domestic violence, my struggle through everyday life, my suffering, and how this experience made me value my relationship with God and the journey to healing and finding self-worth again. I have changed my perspective on the domestic violence I endured. Currently, I use this experience to fuel my life's purpose globally, while leaving my legacy to be continued by helping women of all ages overcome the struggles I endured with domestic violence for over 23 years while being married to a veteran who became more abusive as the years passed. He was able to use PTSD as a crutch to continue the abuse and it became okay and my new norm.

After my separation and 15 years after returning home from the war, Operation Iraqi Freedom, my husband was diagnosed with Anti-Social Personality Disorder. Since his diagnosis, I have learned a lot about our toxic relationship, but most of all I learned about myself. I understand that being an empath, having co-dependent issues, allowed for our 23-year toxic dance.

A background of domestic violence for Alicia

My struggles began in my childhood when I was abandoned by my mother at the tender age of one, enduring an abusive upbringing, then becoming a teen mom by the age of 16, and enduring a lot of cheating and physical abuse at the hands of my first husband, my son's father. My first marriage lasted on- and-off for five years until the age of 21. By the age of 25 I met my second husband while working for an airline as a ticket agent. He was extremely charming, intelligent (he was my on-the-job trainer), and had a funny personality that brightened my day on a daily basis.

He had gone to Basic Military Training which he didn't actively complete, but as the years went by, I wanted him to serve his time to make sure he wouldn't be sought out for going AWOL. (Absent Without Leave in the Military can lead to a conviction and possible jail time). He eventually completed 12 years of part-time Military service and became a veteran after spending a year overseas during Operation Iraqi Freedom.

We shared a total of 23 years of dating and marriage. We had a wonderful friendship as co-workers for six months before our first date. During that time, we enjoyed each other's company very much and we had a lot in common. We both were single parents; he had a 12-month-old daughter and I had a 7-year-old son. We enjoyed traveling, although we had not done much traveling yet, we enjoyed social gatherings, some weekend nightclubs, dancing, a big passion for music.

About 2 months after we met, he came to work distraught over the breakup with his girlfriend at the time (his daughter's mother, as he called her). He said she cheated on him with his best friend and it was questionable if his daughter was even his? He explained that he had loved her since her birth and it didn't matter if she was his daughter or not, but he couldn't remain with the mother anymore and had moved in with his sister whom he had met three years before because his father had about nine children from different women and he was now getting to know his father and his siblings.

We continued as friends, hanging out with our co-workers until one night he asked me out on a date. After a couple of months of dating he seemed very upset. When I asked him if he was ok, he explained that his sister was moving to Massachusetts, which would leave him homeless because he was paying his ex's rent and child support.

By this time, I had fallen deeply in love with him. I was a struggling single parent with a son, and the idea of him moving in temporarily seemed like a great idea. He immediately moved in, but wasn't able to help me in any way financially, which put a huge strain on our relationship and I would often be upset due to his lack of funds and me having to always pay for everything, but I knew we could work through the rough patches and our finances would eventually work out. During a night out clubbing with co-workers, I found out he also had an older son with his high school sweetheart. When I asked him if this rumor was true, he began weeping and explaining that a year after he broke up with his son's mother, she began dating his youngest brother from his father's side (who he met at 18 years old) and she had currently moved away to Connecticut and was expecting a second child with his brother.

He went on to say that she cheated on him with another guy and she was pregnant during the 12 months while he was away at boot camp for the Army. His son was born in Connecticut and paternity was never established. I was totally shocked as my heart melted for him, He didn't see this child because she had moved away with her new live-in boyfriend, which was his younger brother, and she was expecting a second child from his brother. As I watched him in tears, my heart just broke for him. I fell deeper in love as I could relate to being hurt by my ex-husband's (my son's dad) cheating, physically abusive ways.

We discussed paternity for his son and getting his visitation rights with both children. During these discussions, there were times he would put a pillow over his head and began screaming "leave me alone, my kids are none of your business", or he would leave and sleep on the floor or couch. I would explain that this was simply a conversation. I wanted to help him, but his behavior seemed bizarre! Most of the time I would hug him and try to be compassionate and nurturing. Although I was only

25 years old, learning about life, and he was 21, I seemed to be more knowledgeable due to completing my Associate's Degree and having been established and independent since the age of 14. I also knew the family court system, so I assured him everything would work out so he could see his children.

How domestic abuse took away my sanity

About 10 months after he moved in I started noticing the RED FLAGS; his behavior changed, he began coming home late, disappearing often without explanation of his whereabouts until the wee morning hours, leaving for the holidays then responding by shrugging his shoulders if I was upset, saying "it's a feeling, you will get over it".

My intuition began nudging at me, so I decided to check his wallet - I found a key. I didn't question him right away about the key until the night he came home at 5am from his daughter's birthday party (her mother shares the same birthday). During this heated argument, I explained that having a child's birthday party until 5am was unacceptable to me. He responded by saying "it was my daughter's mother's birthday too"! That was my 'aha' moment when it dawned on me that he may be cheating on me while freeloading at my house.

The following day, we sat down to talk like best friends, which we had become. I very lovingly explained that if he wanted to break-up to try and reconcile his family I would understand. I valued the family unit and could never live with being the cause of keeping a family apart. I explained that although it would hurt me, I would prefer his honesty and we could remain cordial friends as well as co-workers. He assured me that I was being silly, he adored me.

Although I tried to ignore what transpired, that weekend remained uneasy for me until one day I decided to call his daughter's mother. I introduced myself as his girlfriend, told her he would be on his way to pick up their beautiful daughter that I had met several times at work since their breakup one year ago. She was shocked, confused, and angry saying they never broke up, and he had just stepped out to go shopping with his daughter!!

I was also completely SHOCKED since he lived with me, but she thought he was living in his sister's house, who had relocated to Massachusetts the prior year. That night when he came home, he was angry and began yelling at me saying "why did you ruin my visitation with my daughter, now I am never going to see her". He began packing his clothes saying that he was leaving. I asked him "how could you be MAD at me when you have been living with me and cheating on me this whole time"? I wept as he threw all his clothes all over my bedroom as he continued yelling and cursing at me.

And that's the first time he pushed me up against the wall as he yelled in my face "you're NOT my mother", as he continued choking me. Streams of tears flowed down my face and my heart sank. I was extremely hurt by his behavior. We all loved him at work, I had always felt like he was the nicest person I have ever met and that he got a raw deal in life just like I did. I couldn't believe the lies and deceit. I was completely heartbroken and felt like a complete fool. Once he had seen my tears streaming down my face, he began weeping and saying he was sorry, explaining "it's just that she will not allow me to see my daughter if she knows I have a girlfriend, and I love my daughter, I want to be in her life".

Being naive and gullible, I began explaining that she couldn't blackmail him into a relationship with her for visitation rights with his daughter because there are laws against that in the family court system that would give him visitation rights. He was only 22 and had no idea about his paternal rights. That night, he left with all his belongings and was living in his car for a couple of days before I took him back in the house. During our break-up period, he kept professing his love for me, swearing he never wanted to be with his ex because she had cheated on him with his best friend, and paternity was questionable with both his children. He convinced me to have another conversation with his ex and confirm his story. She admitted to having a relationship with his friend during a separation period but explained that the rumors were false, and the 2-year-old was, in fact, his daughter.

He said that everything was now out in the open and he wanted a clean slate with us. In my mind, I felt the trust was not only violated, but it was ruined. He continued crying, begging, pleading for my forgiveness because this was true love and we are soulmates. I couldn't resist, we were in love.

A couple of months later we were driving around, and he began weeping saying he was too ashamed to tell me a secret because he was scared that I would leave him. I assured him that I wouldn't leave him ever. I needed him to confide in me so we could rebuild our trust. I cried and begged for him to open up to me! I wanted us to have an unbreakable bond where we can have an open discussion on all topics without it being a hindrance to our relationship status. As he continued crying, he said he was too ashamed to tell me but he had to because he loved me so much and worried about my health. Finally, he said, "she has HPV and we need to both get checked". I was shocked beyond devastated because I had never been exposed to any sexually transmitted diseases.

That night in the car, he agreed to see multiple doctors with me in the examination room so I can ask the doctors all my questions to put my mind at ease. We both agreed if he was infected, the relationship would be over. This was a huge strain on our relationship. But once we were both cleared of NOT having been infected with HPV, both he and the ex assured me their relationship had long been over and she had confessed this secret to him now after many years of hiding it.

Once again, I succumbed to all his tears and pleas that he loved me and we should give it another try. Things became difficult as he was constantly having physical altercations with his ex and she would always call me to be the mediator. I always remained out of their arguments. She finally put an Order of Protection on him and he began picking up his daughter in the presence of a third party. I adored his children early on as they were only 12 months and 2-years-old when I met them (another RED FLAG I ignored. He had both women pregnant at the same time and he was only 21 when we met). We had an instant family. I reached out to his son's mother and we agreed on child support out of court which I set up as auto-pay for him, including some visitation rights as she lived over three hours away.

Since the day we met, he always raved how he admired my independence, intelligence, and motivational drive. He began voicing how he wished he could become successful one day and go to college. We both aspire for a future with financial freedom and children together. He used to joke saying he wanted a football team. I encouraged him to see all the potential he had, convincing him to let me enroll him in the same college I attended. He said he couldn't afford college. I explained how Financial Aid worked and eventually enrolled him.

I began redoing or tweaking my previous homework, term papers, take-home exams from my previous semester for him. I also submitted a request to combine his credits, military experience, and work experience which allowed him to attain a Bachelor's Degree in Business Administration soon after I completed mine.

Throughout these years, he always said he was less than me and how I thought I was better than him. I lived many years training and teaching him everything I knew to make him feel like an equal in the relationship. I wanted us to attain a better life together, for him to become more stable financially by investing in stocks (even if it was 1%), open a checking/savings account.

He dreamed of getting a car from the dealer and I made sure to help him reach that goal, all in hopes that he would see our progress as equals and envision the life we were building together. I had hopes that the more he accomplished the better his self-esteem would become, and he would be less angry and resentful, but that wasn't the case.

As time went on, he began having more and more jealous outbursts, saying he wanted us to move because this was my apartment and neighborhood. I agreed with him that we would move to a more economical neighborhood away from my friends and family. (Isolation another RED flag I missed)

In our new apartment, the fits of rage became more frequent, jokes became crueller, and that's when I believe the gaslighting began. I bought him a keyboard he really wanted for Christmas, which he shattered in a fit of rage because he found old pictures from my previous relationship and ripped them to pieces and scattered them all over the living room while I was at work. My son bought me a frame for Mother's Day and he punched the glass right out, he never had any remorse for his outbursts of rage.

By this time, we had his brothers and one sister residing with us and they were also abusive towards me, all in a joking way. His older brother moved in after being released from prison and began coming home in the morning disturbing my sleep for work the following day. This went on for months while his brother slept all day and when I asked my husband to set boundaries, he simply told his brother that I was being a b**** and didn't want him living in our home anymore. His sister moved in with her daughter, whom she was physically abusing. She wasn't contributing financially, or helping with chores, and wouldn't attend to her 5-year-old daughter.

Every night after work I would come home to take care of all the chores until one day I had a fit of rage myself and began throwing things in the kitchen because of their lack of consideration and not cleaning off the dinner table. My husband walked into the kitchen while his sister slept on the couch after dinner and he laughed at me being upset and shrugged his shoulders as he did so often. Then he smirked at me, went into our bedroom, closed the door, and put the volume up on the Yankee's game so he wouldn't hear my frustration.

This was the first time I acted crazy by pulling the TV out of the wall and flinging it. I immediately realized that my behavior was irrational and put my coat on to go for a car ride. As I began walking out, he slammed me against the door and wouldn't let me move saying "who do you think you are and where are you going?, you're not going anywhere". I was in such a rage that he put his hands on me AGAIN, and I began hitting him back. His sister jumped in and separated us. A little later, she moved to Florida, and once again we broke up for a couple of days.

When we met, he confessed that he had an issue with the Military trainer and was not sure if he had an outstanding warrant for his arrest for being AWOL. After some research, I was able to touch base with someone in the Military that was able to straighten out his paperwork. He would have to complete his Military obligation, which he signed up for after his mother passed away. He explained there were a lot of issues during his teen years with his mother due to her dating his best friend. We cried and bonded when discussing our childhood as I was a product of a teen pregnancy, abandoned by my mother at 1- year-old because she became an intravenous drug user. My father raised me with different stepmothers due to his drinking issues! We seemed to be a MATCH made in HEAVEN! And so continued our codependent relationship and toxic dance.

Before his deployment, we had another breakup due to his wishing my train would derail during my commute. This fit of rage was due to my attending my aunt's funeral and not running to his side because he had a fender bender on the way to the funeral home. Being that we were not married yet, I decided to breakup and have him move out again due to his erratic verbal abuse. During this six-month separation I dated a new guy who became a stalker when I decided to end the relationship.

I was shocked when I found out my ex had physically assaulted this new guy badly! I had never seen him fight and was shocked to see this new guy's face, ribs and body beaten. I couldn't believe he was capable of beating someone up to this extent, especially since he was always the nice guy at work, and everyone loved him. I excused his behavior by thinking that he fought for me out of love. Of course, his revenge was to have protected sex with his daughter's mother so the information would eventually get back at me and hurt me once again.

After six months apart, he came to see me and explained that he may be getting deployed and he wanted to make sure my son and I would be taken care of in case something happened to him. He said he had loved me since the first day he saw me and wanted me to be his wife! I was elated to get married because I believed TRUE LOVE can conquer all, and we would be an example of that. That thinking led me to many days and nights of abuse during my marriage as he became more successful and powerful! He sought revenge and often explained that I had to pay the consequences of hurting him so much during the five years we dated because I kept breaking up with him and I CHEATED ON HIM! He began twisting the events, timelines and never being accountable for all the damage he created since we met. By this time, I was married and committed to spending my life with him, regardless of my CONSEQUENCES!

After getting married, he began using my childhood wounds and information about my parents to keep me feeling ashamed and worthless. He belittled my parenting skills, made fun of me when I lost my employment during 9/11, constantly joked about my habits and appearance in the form of ridicule, and whatever I held dear. I began gaining weight and feeling worthless, forgetting the woman I once was before meeting him. He always denied everything when he was questioned about his behavior. To him, it was all part of his jokes and I just didn't get it because I was too sensitive.

The manipulation and lack of love began suffocating me. I had no idea he continued gas-lighting, my perception of reality started to become blurred under his verbal, emotional, physical abuse. I was caving under the pressure of all the stress. Every so often he would show affection in front of family members to maintain a happy front. He seemed to think that he had the authority and the power to abuse me most of the time. He was an anti-villain, acting nice to everyone around him, making me feel like I was doing everything wrong and he is a nice guy.

He was manipulative and was thriving on my confusion. It was a vicious cycle and it made me feel as though I was truly losing my mind. I was in a hole and there was no escape. This led to me questioning everything from my worth to whatever belonged to me. He continuously accused me of cheating to make him feel like I wasn't fulfilling his sexual desires. He even accused me of being gay because I felt no sexual desire towards him due to all the years of abuse from him and his whole family.

In 2004, he went away to Operation Iraqi Freedom, which he returned from worse; angrier and rageful. We both began working for the same company again after years of different occupations. During these years, he started having jealous fits of rage with several co-workers. I dove into work and helped him move up the success ladder while I remained in a lower level position but began expanding on our real estate portfolio, which he blatantly refused to help manage and would constantly begin daily fights regarding how I managed these properties.

His career was propelled to managing an international airport and charming most woman he encountered at work. We purchased our first house, a two-income property that was a fixer-upper and he constantly created chaos with the repairs saying all I did was get him into a mess. We eventually moved into our second home which was a single-family. He eventually changed the locks and left me homeless. He kept all my belongings, including my two pets, and yelled for me to never come to the house or call him again because I was a no good whore who cheated on him a bunch of times with several co-workers, even with his cousin.

At that point, we also rented an apartment in New York which I was evicted from due to him stealing my tax return documentation. I was left homeless while owning my own homes! I went to the police who, in turn, said there was nothing they could do. I tried to get in the home, but he put cameras up saying he was going to tell the police I was crazy and had abandoned him, which was a lie!! He began telling everyone I ABANDONED HIM!! Not that he BULLIED me out of my OWN HOME. I put all my belongings from the NY apt in storage while I waited several months to receive a settlement cheque from a previous car accident. Although he abandoned me during my recovery from surgery, this accident was my blessing in disguise!!

During those months, I stayed at a hotel, Airbnb's, and with family. It was a very dark couple of years. When I finally received my settlement check, I purchased a foreclosed house with no heat or hot water. I spent that winter sleeping on an air mattress with water only in the sink. I took showers on the back porch during the summer until I was able to fix the plumbing and heating in the house. Even though this was domestic violence in the form of emotional and mental abuse, as well as financial abuse, there was nothing authorities could do.

At that point, I was very sick and was recovering from rotator cuff surgery. Months later, I was alone and in and out of the hospital needing blood infusions for my treatment while suffering from anxiety and I couldn't keep track of things and had memory problems. The anxiety led to stressful behavior at work, as I was very nervous always. I often became irritable, which affected my production at work. I began incurring moving violation tickets while driving and I was written up at work for being combative towards the supervisors because I was always on fight-or-flight mode. My whole life was in chaos, spinning out of control. I became the talk in the hallways at work because everyone looked at me weird. After all, I had a wonderful husband that everyone desired. I soon went back into counselling sessions again to gain clarity!

By this time I had used all my credit cards and ended up in a huge financial mess. I had nothing left but to turn to God and try to fix my life. All my life, I was codependent and trying to fix everything from homes to people, but I never truly loved myself enough to value my own self-worth nor did I require others to respect me. At this point I made me first CODA meeting and felt like I finally found myself!!

I had settled with him wanting to work out my marriage at the cost of myself. Through the years, he refused to join me in counselling, or to put in any effort in resolving our issues. Everything had disintegrated since my multiple miscarriages due to fighting, and his lack of compassion as I lay in bed bleeding for two weeks during another miscarriage. His lies, infidelity, abusive behavior, and his demeaning attitude towards me had taken its toll and wreaked havoc in my mind, body and spirit!

After 2 years of crying in a deep dark depression, I decided to begin learning about self-love, healing every day, having an active prayer life, and becoming a New York State Chaplain, while serving the community by volunteering for multiple Ministries. My new home is still a work in progress.

Step by step, I am starting to rebuild my life and move forward while dealing with the painful memories, and all the lies he continues to say in the courthouse while trying to steal all my properties I diligently worked for without his support. My divorce has been a harsh reality that I was married to a complete stranger all these years. Now my dream is to educate and empower women globally who are being abused in any capacity. I encourage you to leave abusive relationships and learn to love yourself again through God's eyes. Regain your faith and know that God will see you through everything!

When it came to domestic abuse, I always associated it with physical harm or bruises. As a cycle that would repeat itself daily, sort of like my first marriage. I had a black eye, a busted lip, black and blue that I could look at and see the signs of domestic violence. My first husband partied and disappeared on weekends with other women. The abuse was consistent and evident. In this case, I wasn't really aware of it being truly domestic violence since the physical violence towards me was once every couple of years. He would always say I didn't understand the joke, or I was too serious, took things way too personally. Growing up in a dysfunctional family, I always felt like I was a bit crazy. Once I confided this to my husband, he began using this against me by saying I was the crazy one who needed medication. He convinced me to begin medication, I didn't realize he was the major cause of my anxiety and inner FEAR Since I didn't even know the definition of gaslighting or its effects. He made me feel tremendous guilt any times I acted out of character in self-defense by stooping down to his level and raising my hands and engaging in physical abuse to defend myself.

The lines became blurred as to who was the problem, me or him? My husband led me to believe I needed mental help for many years. My psyche always made excuses for his bad behavior towards me because I was the only person who saw any flaws in him. The outside world adored him. Co-workers, family members, and friends often reminded me of how lucky I am to be married to *such a good guy*. How could they all be WRONG and I was the ONLY ONE RIGHT? I needed more MEDS ... OMG ... I am going NUTS!

Holding onto the past

As the years went by, my husband continuously reminded me of all the mistakes I had ever made during our relationship. These reminders made me feel guilty and it allowed him to make sarcastic comments, berate and belittle me without me ever objecting or putting any boundaries. I often held onto the good times we shared, disregarding his past mistakes. For years, I just dove into work, purchasing real estate, being a landlord, planning for our children, and putting on a show of our perfect life in front of family/friends. I continuously apologized whenever he had fits of rage to make things work. I often took the blame for everything or anything to make life easier, less stressful. I kept conversations light, surface level. He often said I was not self-sufficient enough to fulfill my wifely duties in the kitchen or the bedroom which made me feel worthless, insecure, and unlovable.

Gaslighting

Hmmm ... gaslighting...what is that? A word I learned after separation which made everything become clear!! The FOG was lifted!

Wikipedia definition is:

Gaslighting is a form of psychological manipulation in which a person seeks to sow seeds of doubt in a targeted individual or members of a targeted group, making them question their own memory, perception, or sanity. Using denial, misdirection, contradiction, and lying, gaslighting involves attempts to destabilize the victim and delegitimize the victim's beliefs.

I began questioning my sanity before we were even married due to my husband's gaslighting/lying to me for years. The gaslighting began with verbal abuse, mocking my appearance and my weight then denying he ever said it. He would always respond by saying "you are crazy I would never treat you like that. I love my wife, but she needs help". "My wife is a cuckoo bird, but I love her". During a visit from his younger cousin, he humiliated me by saying I needed stitches down there because he couldn't feel anything during sex. When I addressed him, crying over how humiliated I felt, he kept repeating "you're a liar. I would never say that to my wife, I love my wife".

Whenever I became angry or questioned him, he would always call me crazy and an overly sensitive person who wasn't fun enough to get his jokes. If I asked, "why did the joke always have to be about me"? he would say "OMG why are you so sensitive?". He would move things and hide my belongings, as he sat back and watched me go crazy searching for the things he hid. I remember his smirk and his sinister raised eyebrow as he enjoyed watching me struggle, search in desperation.

Taking control of everything

A year into our relationship, he began saying we should move because he didn't feel comfortable living in my neighborhood and he felt the apartment belonged to me. He suggested we move to OUR place. I totally understood his feelings and we moved but I always missed my old neighborhood, my friends. He often fought over me having my own bank account, saying if we are married I should be completely transparent. Because my first husband left me homeless, I always explained that I had to have a separate account for my son's needs. He said

I was never fully invested in the marriage and had trust issues! This account had funds I had acquired before meeting him from a car accident when I was younger. This caused him to throw things in fits of rage during the marriage while screaming "Alicia always needs a get out of jail free card".

Upon his return from Iraq, he claimed he didn't want to live in New York anymore. During that time, my son was doing very poorly in school and was becoming a troubled teen so we decided to relocate to a rural area in Pennsylvania. Once I was isolated in Pennsylvania, he began fighting whenever I was talking on the phone. He would argue if I wanted to visit family and friends in New York. He also began saying I had lesbian affairs with my girlfriends and that's why I always wanted to visit them and never have sex with him. Little by little, I had less contact with people, my life became about pleasing him to avoid his fits of rage and breaking things, punching holes in walls, or chocking me.

Infidelity and accusations

If I was ever seen talking to a co-worker or received any communication from a male, he would automatically break my cell phone. (He BROKE MANY since I work in a male-dominated environment). He broke computers after hacking into my Facebook and seeing I had male friends. He was always frustrated, angry, or raging at home. He showcased me as a crazy person who was driving him crazy with my obsessions and my weird controlling behavior anytime we were in the company of friends and family. He would often use these excuses to not speak to me or break up and leave for a few days, which would trigger me to constantly try and prove my innocence or beg to save our marriage.

He was the expert in projecting things and making up stories. I caught him speaking to women at all hours and if I questioned him, he would call me crazy. Several women called and said he was having affairs with them and he would always convince me that it was his ex trying to break us up. His phone always remained with an empty call log because he claimed it would slow his phone down. Ninety percent of his calls came in as private or blocked, which he would never answer and if I questioned him, he would say "I don't answer those kinds of calls, you answer it". Anytime I picked up one of those calls, the caller would always hang up, which led me to believe the women he had affairs with understood he was married. My gut always felt like he was committing adultery while accusing me of infidelity with multiple men during our marriage.

The silent treatment and offensive body language

He often would shut down and nothing was up for discussion as he ignored me for days while sleeping with his back turned towards me. I remember how he used to stare at me in disgust. He would roll his eyes, look up with his arms crossed, and always answer my questions or concerns with "oh, boy, here we go again". "Whatever". "I don't care". "You will get over it". "Yes, yes Dr, Phil, that's why no one likes you, you think you're a brainiac". "That's why your ex-husband beat you, because of that mouth of yours". "You never know how to apologize, learn how to be humble like me". "I am the only asshole that would deal with your crazy ass", being that my cooking talent is very weak he would often say "I need a wife that can cook, no man is going to deal with you not cooking".

Grabbing the fat around my stomach became his regular joke saying how he remembered when we met, he could barely grab fat and now it's a whole handful. I slowly stopped wearing sexy things to bed and began covering my body more due to shame. There were times he refused to have sex saying he was tired, or I neglected him so much in the past he is no longer in the mood. I often cried, begging us to get counselling and he would respond by saying "stop diagnosing me, you don't have a degree in psychology".

How my misfortune took the right turn

For five years I struggled with life at every front. From being evicted, homeless, and being ridiculed affected me at work because my husband was a supervisor in my company and used his fellow co-workers to harass and make up issues to write me up. He had gained everyone's sympathy by going to work, crying and falsely making up horrific lies. He told co-workers one day after work he came home and found me in bed with another man but forgave me!! My personal and professional life hit rock bottom during this time, I felt my whole life being pulled out from under me. My husband changed the locks to my home, and I was staying in hotels, Airbnb's, and family members' houses until I was able to get back on my feet.

With no home, no comfort, and no peace of mind, I continued calling upon God to overcome the toxicity. I began to invest in the woman I had lost so many years ago. It began with learning what emotional wellness was by taking a class on a basic and advanced level. I had no idea that emotional intelligence was actually a thing. This self-awareness and self-growth approach allowed me to rebuild my self-confidence/self-worth. During this time, I have traveled to many places which helped bring me back to life, allowed me to meet diverse people, experience growth on many levels, and spark a passion inside me to raise awareness about domestic violence.

The journey back from my dark night of the soul to my brighter days

I cried out to the Lord on many nights during this transition seeking God's love, wisdom, and blessings. I begged and pleaded with God to salvage my marriage. It took many years of fighting against the obvious. Once I realized the marriage was unsolvable, I began praying for my strength and inner healing as I continue finding wisdom and purpose from my life's journey. Although I still have difficult days, I often remain in close relationship with God, reading the bible and surrounding myself with like-minded people. This continually replenishes my soul and motivates me to push past all the trauma as I continue to remain a kind, loving human being, free from toxic relationships, anger, bitterness, or hatred. I remind myself daily that I am not who my ex-husband or people label me to be. I understand this comes from their perspective and that hurting people hurt people. I have grown to understand that when an anointed woman has a purpose, she usually faces great challenges, pain, and suffering to be stretched and grown. She must overcome to learn endurance which allows for her greater purpose.

Although I am still in the chaos of divorce, I continue to work on self-love and move the needle a little closer to fulfill my life's passion. I trust in God's plan with an unshakeable faith in Him.

Chapter 8

Qoqo Love

The perfect balance between yin and yang, the space in the middle and the circle around. An overcomer, actualizer, and self-care steward. Known as original Beauty Divine DNA, 'In my presence, you remember and know who You are'. Qoqo Love became an ordained Minister in 2019 at the University of Metaphysics in Sedona. A Priestess, a Warrior, a Healer, and a Self-proclaimed Resurrector. Her motto is to "Redefine Welfare because being Well is Fair".

While traveling to Guyana, she noticed the abundance from the air and declared "Poverty by design is Intentional and Poverty by Nature is Impossible". Now knowing that domestic violence, poverty, and poor housing are symptoms and by-products of a construct. This fueled a quest in her to

141

approach life, living from the inside out, Out Loud. Born Angela to James and Stella in 1964 when the world was once again on its head about many of our current issues. She cultivated "Qoversations with Qo" embracing racial matters, health disparities, women's issues, poverty dynamics, and the right to be well. During the civil rights era, Malcolm X said, "the most unprotected woman in America was a black woman and domestic violence was her number one enemy". As a Cross-Cultural Communicator, she now knows this statement to transcend culture, economic status, and ethnic backgrounds.

Studied Transformative and Leadership and Social Change at Maryland University of Integrated Health MA, holds a BA in Business Administration at Sojourner Douglass College, and a Certified Breathologist. Creating Healing Family CirclesCommunity
Q3 Qommunity Qollective Qommerce.

QoQo Love

Transformative Leadership and Social Change

Q3 Qreative Qollective Qommerce

Dedicated that I could

God/Goddess

Twitter QoQo Love

Instagram: QomisaDesigns

Facebook: QoQo Love

Website: QoQoLove.com

LinkedIn: QoQo Love

For the past 6 years, after a series of traumatic events, QoQo has spent her time in introspection, contemplation, and meditation. Developing her acumen for the five elements of oneness with nature, spirituality, and mindfulness practices, using these and other methodologies to transform her own life. In 2020, her team will launch Stellar Notte' a (501c3) non-profit in honor of her mother, Stella, with an exhibition, "Invisible in Plain Sight". Exploring the impact of health care disparity, supremacy, poverty, and the politics of self-care in marginalized communities.

Dear Mia and Sache'

The Cloak of Silence to Sacred Being by QoQo Love

One of my earliest and happiest memories of myself is on the front lawn at my father's house in Fort Pierce, Florida. I'm outside and the sun is shining brightly. It appears to be Sunday or a Special Sunday like Easter. My dress is yellow like a lemon yellow. There is a green bow and I have on black patent leather shoes and white frilly socks. My skin is deep dark mocha brown, my teeth are bright, and my eyes are glistening like stars. I can feel myself swirling endlessly. The smile on my face seems to radiate from my entire body as if I'm the sun and its rays are radiating from me. I miss so many things about her freedom and her innocence.

143

As a pre-teen in New York, life is good. My cousins are here and my friends and I run track and take photography classes. I go to the modelling studio with my cousin regularly and I'm known as the Pied Piper of the younger children, and my nickname is Smiley. At some point, we move back to Baltimore, and life is not quite the same. I never seemed to integrate as I did in New York. However, it is in Baltimore that I had a vision about who I was to be in the world. A wealth Ambassador for my family, to take them out of poverty to prosperity. At 19, I buy my first house for my mother. I study real estate and money as a hobby. Something about me is free. I'm living from the inside out.

Though I never saw, or don't remember seeing, my father physically hurt my mother. The pain of what she experienced still haunts me today.   My mother was a 3rd grade-educated woman born March 17, 1936. She did all that she could do and that was to pack up her three small children 12, 6, and 2 and move them across the country from Florida to Baltimore, then New York, and then back to Baltimore. Here is where I feel the connection to my mother in looking at her life. She never rose to her fullest potential. She was a middle child just like me. She had a charm and pizzazz that was unparalleled to her upbringing She wanted to be a world-class gospel singer. Unfortunately, with no education and no skills, we moved 18 times and three states before I was 18 years old. We were raised on Welfare, never having enough food or clothes regularly.   Honestly, this made it difficult for me to connect with people at a deeper level. This, perhaps, was the basis of my vision to be a wealth ambassador for my family.

I spent several years trying to figure out what was it about me that attracted this abuse in my life. I was loving, caring, free, and giving. How could someone who says they love you hurt you? So below is a journal entry of me finally getting it out of my system. It is my hope and desire that all of my children, as well as men and women around the world, will benefit from my story. It is my belief that hurt people hurt people so I'm not here to villainize anyone, only to usher in healing from the inside out.

Today is January 31, 2018. It is the first blue moon in 150 years since 1868 and I'm in California. Who was here? What was here? How does that times' influence dictate what is happening now?

I awoke around 4 am to a text from my daughter Mia with a reminder about the blue moon and to go see it if I could because it was only visible from the East Coast. I jumped up immediately and saw the transition. I returned back to my room and there was another text from a friend giving me a specific time, so I got dressed again and returned. It was beautiful. I returned to my room excited about the possibilities and decided to take a vow of silence.

I dedicate the day to writing and flushing out all that I can. I'm at the Optimum Health Institute in San Diego, California. I have a health crisis; the pain of life has fully expressed itself in my left breast.   My first appointment was a colonic, so I decided to start after that. Wonderful decision. I met Melissa from

North Carolina, a bright and shining star who shared her story of pain, triumph, and transformation. She is a fifty-one-year-old white female who left home on a road trip for two weeks to find herself after a broken heart. (Her husband cheated with a 16-year-old.) On a cliff eight weeks later and talking to God, "You led me here, now what"? she said, after doing things the same way with the same results (same man, different name), she surrendered. She is now happier than she has ever been in her entire life. Hearing her story inspired me to finally face the pain of my own story.

I then proceeded to the office for my Badge to take a "Vow of Silence". Attended a release ceremony. I had two things to release - self-sabotage and an unhealthy body. In my left hand was represented the old stories of shame, of guilt, not being supported, not being loved, not being allowed to be seen, oppressed, suppressed constructs yada, yada, yada, and the impact of not living in my highest potential. No connection to the little girl in the yellow dress. The right hand represented the part I played, the self-sabotage, the negative self-talk, the accepted outside influence. The agreement and participation. I declared after the ceremony to embrace optimum health in my full body, mind, spirit, and environment.

I embrace my beautiful, sexy, kind, generous, giving, wise, loving, free, sacred self into full throttle embodiment. I am here, alive, vibrant, and audacious living my life out loud from the inside out. Thank you, Goddess. I embrace and commit to self-acceptance and surrender. I don't have to be or do anything to have all that is mine. The universe, God,

Angels, messengers, guides, friends, etc. support me, Yes me. I have all that I need right now.

After the colonic and the release ceremony, I find a quiet spot and begin to write, allowing myself to feel and remember things I had blocked out for years, some of my most painful memories.

26-27. It is 1989-1991 I am married, and it is the first time I have experienced depression. My husband has come home to tell me something. I say to him I can deal with anything other than you having someone else pregnant. And that's exactly what he said. Mind you, I was six months pregnant. We were 26 and she was 18. Someone who lived near his aunt's house where he spent a lot of time. This was the same time that I found out from his aunt about his father whom he did not know. Before telling him, I attempted to confirm the information myself.

We did it together, looked up the name we were given, and went there together. We found his grandfather instead and later went to meet his father. In the interim, he was very angry with me. Even violent. In retrospect, I was the closest thing to him, so he took it out on me. This time was filled with so much anger, pain, and abuse. I isolated myself because there was the drug life, money, women, cars, and constant turmoil. I was so depressed I retreated. I was the mother of a 3-year-old and pregnant. The shame, the embarrassment, the women, the friends, the associates, the hairstylist, the dancers, and the performers. His mother holding space for the trickery. Why? How come she wasn't a woman too? From the time I was 18 to 37, and long after divorce, there were 19 plus years of abuse, lies, and deceit. What I recall about this period the most was wanting it to be ok and it never was. Every time I forgave him, it would be something else or someone else.

It turns out that his father did the same thing to his wife. He had an affair with my ex-husband's mother when he was married with two children. He is now his father. Every year is another child coming out of the woodwork saying, "he's my father" and still I tried to hold on, to wait, to pray to be better, to turn the other cheek. All to no avail. My heart was with him because I knew his source of pain. He was just acting out and I thought I could endure. Until he went to prison and while going to visit him, the driver called me someone else's name. He was in jail still doing the same thing. Again, the embarrassment.

The letters, the cards became no more than artwork. I admired the ingenuity and creativity of the inmates to repurpose and create amazing things. He's coming home from prison and I'm shopping, buying gifts. I take too long. He's angry when I get home and he pushes me in front of the girls. "I'm done. I declare that I cannot and will not raise my children this way". I plan my exit strategy. I get a part-time job to save up money and find a place and move. That is the last time we shared space, but not the last time for trauma drama.

All I know is I closed the world out and took care of my children and worked. Dreamed, planned, and existed. I believed in the back of my mind, hoping, praying, that one day we would be a family again. Wife wounded my identity, my purpose, my love, my

148

body, my life. Never really dealing with the effects of abuse, I became silent. I became a shell of an existence. It's here that the shadow of hiding began. I couldn't let anyone know me. I felt that I was protecting my children from the outward effects of the infidelity. Taking pictures, I probably became the most vulnerable. I was always afraid that when we were out someone would come running up to him saying, "Daddy, Daddy". That never happened and yet it played out in many other ways.

Fast forward, the last straw was to witness my daughter experiencing something similar. "I call you, you question me, and go back to sleep". That was the final straw. At that moment, my heart cracked wide open and I have no respect and no love for you. "You f***** me over for most of my adult life. Not protecting me and leaving me vulnerable to your choices. And now, here is our daughter who needs her father, and you don't show up. I am livid and yet I don't hate you. Why? Why, because I can't, I won't. You have your own demons". My mother taught me to love and respect the father and never talk against him. The children would develop their own relationship.

And honestly, this made me relive all the painful years. I felt that I had failed. Children know way more than we give them credit for. More recently, I'm on a date with my daughter and she tells me that someone reached out to her to say her father was their daddy. Yes, I felt it. I haven't really spoken to him since. Trust, exposure, Illusion, deceit, cloaking, weight gain, physical scars, overachieving, get over it, Christian church isolation, retreat, isolation, retreat.

149

327

On March 27, 2013, my life changed forever. I was riding to work where I had traveled every day for the past 13 years. An officer pulls me and says I ran a stop sign. After running my license, then he says my license is suspended and proceeded to arrest me. My oldest daughter was in the car with me and I begged the officer to let my daughter drive, and I would go straight to MVA to find out what this situation was. The officer refused. Somehow, on this day, I knew my life would never be the same. It wasn't just the arrest. It was its timing. You see, I was interviewing at a University for a Director's position and my salary would have almost doubled. I was looking at a beachfront property and everything was about to change for the better. The vision of being an Ambassador of Wealth to take my family out of poverty to prosperity was here. I was going to cross the tracks.

It looked like the struggle was going to be over. It was a ticket from several years ago while traveling through Virginia. The ticket was paid and never corrected in the system. I was so heartbroken in the cell that I refused to eat or drink. Earlier in 2010, right after burying my father, I was diagnosed with DCIS in situ stage 0 unidentified calcifications in my breast, so a mastectomy was suggested. Someone on the team said the medical system refused and they harassed me with phone calls to schedule surgery.

At this point in the cell, my whole life is coming to a head. Fighting for my life because I can feel, internally, that it is all starting to get to me. The childhood, the abuse, the death of my mother, and the prejudice at work. I feel like a time bomb. And so it happened in the cell, on my left breast, the skin cracked around my nipple. And bled.

Now the darkness begins. My breast is slowly rotting away, or my internal pain is eating its way through my flesh. So, on this metal bed with all these voices around me, the officers laughing in the background, the number of women arrested for frivolous things like taking her boyfriend's cell phone three years ago. It was as if the precinct had a finance meeting and wondered how they can generate some quick revenue. As I recall, there wasn't anyone in there who had killed someone or assaulted anyone, they were frivolous charges.

So, from March 27-November 2016. It was trauma after trauma, as well as going through menopause and I didn't know it. My sister and a best friend died. I was arrested two more times for the same issue, the second time at home in front of my baby and, lastly, in front of my temple. For the same ticket. It felt like during the enslavement period when the slave master would do things in front of the other slaves to make an example. It felt, at times, like someone had picked my name out of a hat.

Just before all this, I had enrolled in the Tai Sophia Institute, now the Maryland University of Integrative Health. In fact, the week I was arrested was one of my cohort weeks. I missed the class. As the

University was going through changes, one of the Deans wrote me up as an example to discipline me. I was too ashamed to share what had happened. And yet, I knew I was being made an example of. I used the class as therapy. After the initial cohort, I began to descend all the while fighting to not disappear.

I then headed out to do my research for my thesis, "Redefining Welfare, because Being Well is Fair". This took me on a journey South where I ran into an opportunity to buy a gas station convenience store. I spent another year fighting an establishment that makes room for every other culture race group but a black woman. I finally gave up and came home and got into the bed. I came out long enough to finish my graduate work and then went back in as I was now defeated.

What's interesting in retrospect is my level of fight. I had been fighting my whole life and during this period I did not have it in me. It was all about what was being done to me. When your reserves are down, when you have given so much, when no one notices that you are disappearing in plain sight, when the good Christian Negro Woman construct has nowhere to pray, where do you go, what do you do?

Wasn't she a woman? How come, wasn't she a woman too? It's the Christian way to turn the other cheek.

You retreat and you go into silence and all the pain, the confusion, anxiety, unknowing dreams, unfulfilled character assassination manifests itself into cancer. While participating in a women's circle, I had a death experience. I could no longer hide the undercurrent of my aloofness. The reason I couldn't connect more deeply or intimately was because I was hiding something. I was hiding a breast that now was visibly out of control. All the work I had done keeping myself well was beyond my reach. I had an open wound that covered the complete areola and the nipple was inverted and unrecognizable. In the sanctity of this women's circle, I revealed this to my sisters. I cried deeply mostly because I was relieved. A big burden was lifted.

Even the shame. Why didn't I just go to the doctors? Well, because I was afraid. I could not trust them. They wanted to take my breast off when it was not necessary, and they would not offer me the help I needed like a nutritionist and a therapist until after they cut off my breast. And I didn't because when my sister transitioned, I fell down the stairs and went to the doctors to have my back checked out and ended up in the psych ward because I was filled with grief. I didn't because I received an unnecessary surgery for my gall bladder that left a horrendous scare on my stomach when another technology could have been used. And for many other ancestral reasons that seem to flow through me like the story of Henrietta Lacks.

Nonetheless, I was now exposed. And it felt good and scary. I would have to do something about it. And I did. In January, I went to Optimum Health Institute to detox and rebuild my immune system, and I began Chemo in March of 2018.

Prayer for the Abuser

There are way worse stories of violence and pain than mine and yet when your little girl is silenced, when the cons you have of yourself become a figment of your imagination, and when the very pain of your past becomes the reality of your children in the present, it is something to contend with. It's where the past meets the present and the present dictates your future. I pray for all involved: the illegitimate child, the wounded wife, the stepson, the ex-husband, the grandchildren, no one wins. May we all find peace and harmony, forgiveness, reconciliation, and a way to make our lives matter for our greater good.

Closing

I Q&A I am the question and the answer. In this incarnation, I am a wombman, mother, grandmother, sister, friend, author, and metaphysician minister, Taoist, breathologist, healer, and as a good friend says, I'm a lot of things. However, what I am not is a punching bag, a slave, property, a secretary, or a bed wench.

I am QoQo Love, an activator, actioner, contemplator, and self-actualization specialist. I am QoQo Love, guardian, and governess of Angela L. Hodge-Jones. I am QoQo Love, founder and CFO of Stellar Notte' creating Stars after the night of life.   On October 31, 2019, I founded Stellar Notte', a non-profit organization dedicated to night stars, those people who have experienced trauma, domestic violence, and financial ruin due to ignorance, greed, and insecurity.

Our mission is to empower them to be the best version of themselves by equipping them with the necessary tools and resources to lift themselves up from poverty to prosperity with Financial Literacy, Safe Housing, Spiritual Awareness, and other life skills training.

Chapter 9

Survivor

The Caged Child

When we read the stories of women who live with domestic abuse, our first inner reaction is to ask, "why does she not leave"? That 'why' has accompanied me for more than a third of my life. Why don't I leave? I saw it all. I was raped in my marital bed. I was beaten black and blue when I was five months pregnant. I was humiliated every single day, behind closed doors and in front of people. I have heard it all, all kinds of insults and words that are still deeply engraved in my soul; whore, filth, good for nothing, drama queen, bitch. And it goes on and on.

The Caged Child

I lived with the fear of my life being taken away from me for more than a decade, lying in bed, heart racing, sweat pouring from my armpits whilst my ex-husband lay snoring beside me. And the ever-present question was there - why don't I leave?

When I did finally leave with my whole heart shattered at having busted my family, I still spent hours and hours questioning myself. Did I do right to leave? It haunted me to look in my child's eyes and carry the guilt of having taken her family from her. The lingering doubts that maybe had I been better I would have had a good marriage. I spiralled down and down.

Drink became my escapism. Pain was continuous. I had become a single parent. I was alone. I was a woman who had f****d up big time. I had forgotten the reasons why I had left. The blues and the greens speckled on my skin. I had forgotten the hooded look when I said something that did not please him and what would ensue after. All I could see, live, and think was that I was not good enough. I was selfish.

I had forgotten the drunken rages, the smashing of things, his late nights out with his friends, and him returning home to simply climb on top of me and have his way. I did not know then and not for a very long time that that was rape. I thought it was his due. He was my husband.

I was young when I left him. I left because of the palpable feeling that he would kill me motivated me to rush out. I took it for ten years. Little did I know that the relationship after him was going to be even worse.

Like an addict rushing to her dose, I fell right into it. Another narcissist who charmed me, courted me, wined and dined me. A snake who reeled me in with the sob story of their past, so similar to mine. Someone who seemed to need me, who needed my daughter, and was looking for a family. It only took six months for the pattern to start emerging. The hooded looks, the snarls, and the quick apologies after. The criticism. The hurtful words that were so familiar. So well known. The quick slaps here and there and the flowers sent as a redemption.

We had a restaurant business together. I would take care of everything in the hope I would win approval. I would be the only one serving during the busy nights as it cut expenses, going up and down a spiral staircase carrying heavy plates. I would be shouted at, ridiculed, and have things thrown at my head if I was not quick enough. Clients would leave me little courage notes written hastily on the napkins and hidden under the dirty plates. I would do the accounts, clean, change menus, serve, while also coping with a full-time job and my child. The anger tantrums escalated. They grew worse. No words will ever cover the pain of the loss of myself.

Until the day came when I faced death squarely in the face. After a huge row, after a truly busy night, I just crumpled on the floor, on my knees whimpering, and the snake just came in front of me and hit me with a punch in the face that broke my nose. Blood spurted like a river. I was left alone on the floor, till I called my father who then took me to the ER.

No one asked how it had happened. Not my parents, not the nurses. No one saw anything amiss. As I lay in the hospital bed that night staring at the ceiling my heart was throbbing in tandem with my face. I could not even cry properly; my face was so swollen. Once again, I had hit rock bottom. Once again, I had to think of my child. I had left her father after all, but it was not any easier.

But leave I did. The crazy thing is that both kept running after me, wanting me back for years after I had left. The crazy thing is I was always tempted to go back. Somehow, deep inside, there is a part of you that believes that things could change. They do not.

After that hospital incident, I took the next courageous step. It was the biggest step of all. I started therapy. I took it seriously. Attended all my appointments. I started reading books about abuse and about psychology. Slowly I was making sense and piecing myself together. One session at a time, I was revealing layers of myself that ran deep. Too deep. Until one day I ran into a book called Daughters of Narcissistic Mothers, and that is when the penny finally fell. The light bulb lit within me.

I had tolerated all the abuse for years in all my relationships because from a very young age, that was all I knew. Until I read the book, I never had questioned my upbringing and how my mother had behaved towards me. I was horrified and my memories of my childhood completely incinerated.

But the truth, as ugly and hard as it was to accept, was that. I was beaten black and blue as a girl. I was punished, ridiculed, and closed in rooms. I was starved, compared to, and was never good enough. We call it child abuse, but what it truly is, is a training, a grooming phase which prepares you for the domestic abuse that is to come.

I looked back at all the times I had wanted to leave as a child. I was the caged child (my nickname to myself). How I minutely fantasized each detail of my great escape at 18. Which I did. To fall straight again into a cage. Differently gilded but constraining, demeaning, humiliating just the same.

I looked back and realised that only three people in my life made me sweat under the armpits. My ex-husband, my ex-boyfriend, and my mother. That kind of sweat which smelt of a cornered, hunted animal. That was the day I finally broke free. Mentally I started soaring above all the trauma and pain. I started working fervently on myself. On my healing. On accepting that it was NOT MY FAULT. And that was Power. A powerful release. Not just from the past but also from the stigmatised image I had of myself.

The healing brought the transformation. From victim and abused, I became motivated. I had sworn to help women. To be there for women who, like me, have gone through the claws and razors of abuse. I can say I am healed. But, like a diabetic person, I still carry within me all the scars and shadows. I have turned them into tools. To know what I deserve, to know what I want, and to carve my own path towards my own happiness.

Many books helped me in my healing phase. I am hoping that this story too, which you are reading right now with my words, can be a beacon of light and hope.

Reach out!

There is always help.

Leave when your gut tells you to.

Love yourself because regardless of what you have been told

You are amazing

You are unique

You are just perfect the way you are.

Chapter 10

Survivor

Reborn

I grew up in Malta in an ardent Catholic family who believed very deeply in the Catholic values and traditions. My parents took us to Mass every Sunday and being kind and respectful to others was very important. I also have an uncle who is a Priest, who has also been an influence in my upbringing.

I met my husband abroad when I was reading for a Master's Degree in the medical field. He was very charming and funny and had so much energy. Until then, I had never met anyone like him before, in fact, he stood out from the rest. He courted me with a bunch of flowers every month at work and surprise trips abroad. He was so charming I fell in love through and through. We had things in common as we did the same job, but were so different in many other ways, mainly different cultures and religions.

After a few months, he gave me a ring that looked like an engagement ring and I refused it, thinking this was too early and I did not want to rush things. We did quite a bit of travelling together. We both worked hard and earned a fair amount of money which enabled us to enjoy life together. At that point in time, we seemed to have the same goals in life. We both wanted a large family, it all seemed like it was meant to be. We dated for three years and then got married. We had a dream wedding with no expense spared. I remember the speech at our wedding sounded like it was out of a movie. I remember everyone telling me how they had never seen anyone so happy to get married and how romantic everything was.

Unexpectedly, as soon as we got back from our honeymoon, there was a shift in behaviour. He started having some major problems at work. I remember one of his friends coming to our house almost every night helping him to write letters on legal matters and giving him advice about how to deal with his problem. His best friend used to tell me "my goodness, he's very depressed". So, I really tried my best to make life easy for him. All the positive energy he had started becoming negative, drowning him on the sofa every night with a tub of ice cream, and putting him in the lowest of moods. But I thought that was ok as marriage is full of ups and downs and therefore it would pass. I remember getting a phone call from him while I was at the supermarket saying he needed £40k to get free from his work contract. I didn't bat an eyelid and lent him the money thinking things would get better then.

But they did not, and the money was never returned.

Things were getting progressively worse and more aggressive, extremely intimidating, but never actually physical. Every time he got back from work he would be sitting on the sofa with his laptop 'working'. I would just ask a simple question like "how was your day?" and it would end up with him getting angry and shouting, either because a client had complained or because an employee was not doing well enough for him. I remember clearly once asking "what time do you start work tomorrow?" and he just shouted "go and check on the software, don't keep asking me these stupid questions! I have work to do!".

It got to the point where we literally stopped communicating. It was a miserable life with things getting more and more aggressive. Every time I would try to ask what the problem was or how we could make things better, it would end up becoming a barrage of "it's all in your mind", "you're making a fuss ", or, "I'm stressed with work", followed by a large amount of abuse and aggressive behaviour.

Things were different whenever we were in the company of other people. If we had a special occasion like a party at his friend's house, he would try and seem like he is the life and soul of the party, the funniest guy in the house, and the most loving husband. It was all an act that I had lived too often.

Once, I was at one of these weekend gatherings with his friends and I just mentioned that the business was not very busy to a friend of mine. I did not think anything of it until we got into the car on the way back home and he started yelling "you never tell people that business isn't good" and "watch what you say, you ask me first!". That day I felt like, oh my goodness. I can't even say what I think now? Every day felt like I was treading on eggshells. What mood is he going to wake up in? What were today's requests? One day it would be looking for socks, one day bank cards or keys. I remember thinking to myself, how can someone wake up so angry ALL the time?

There was one friend I confided in because I trusted she would know I was not lying or making things up. I felt that if I had told any of my old friends they would think "what on earth are you doing staying in an abusive relationship like that?" and they would not understand. She told me that this was not normal and that this behaviour should be unacceptable. I used to keep asking her "am I the one going mad"? because I started doubting myself so much that I needed to hear it from an outsider.

Still in love and hopeful, I then fell pregnant. I was happy because I had always wanted children and I wondered how it would be. We had a son and in the first few days, I realised straight away that my husband was not able to look after him. I could not trust the baby would be safe with him. He was too distracted and always on his phone. His needs came before the baby's and I would say the relationship went downhill from there.

We had several crisis moments like when he just went off and bought a new house without telling me, or a motorbike, or a new business, or going off on several holidays with his friends and not telling me until the day before, or making whole scenes of humiliation in front of friends staying over with us. The list was endless. Our marriage was not teamwork. It was HIS show and I had to accept it. Between friends, when relating these events everyone would find these things funny and far-fetched. But they were my reality and they were awful. But the worst thing of all is that I could not share the pain. I had to pretend we were doing great until I could get home and cry myself to sleep while writing him letters asking for changes in an attempt to rescue our relationship, and there were many!

But then you excuse it because everyone knows that when you have young children it can be hard for a couple. Especially because we were definitely not pulling on the same rope and we were no team. He was focused on his business and money, and I was focused on the children full time because I had no option but to stop work for their early years.

I tried different coping strategies like attending a mindfulness course. Over the years, on my insistence, we had tried marriage counselling a few times. I remember as soon as we would walk in the room he would just laugh and say, "I know I am the problem here". I remember one counsellor told me "I am throwing two cushions in front of you. Imagine your life with him in 20 years, imagine your life without him in 20 years". And I was shocked. How dare someone suggest that I would not be with him. But the reality was that I knew. Deep down, I knew what I needed to do, it was just that I lacked the courage to do it. I was torn between the 'marriage is for life' mantra and the reality of the situation which was that this man did not love me. He loved himself more than anything and the children and I were just an appendage for his social status.

On the second visit to a different counsellor, my husband said to me, "I'm not paying for this nonsense. Just say we are ok now and we've found ways to deal with our issues". So, I did. I lied about how amazing things were now and that we did not need any more sessions. He told me he has never seen any couple solve things so quickly. If only he knew the truth.

I used to tell my friend who I had confided in that I felt like I was in a prison with chains around my ankles. Very rarely, because I could not trust him looking after the children, I used to go to her house for a cup of tea and a chat. Sure enough, I knew that if I had told him ahead of time, he would come home with some sort of urgent thing that needed doing.

One time he wanted me to pack his bags for a work trip he had. I remember a full-blown argument with lots of insults and shouting because I did not see him off properly. It was literally like a toddler tantrum. I was so exhausted from trying to reason with him and the fact that I knew he was doing this to spoil my evening with my friend, that by the time I did get to my friend's house I was too tired to even enjoy my time with her and went back home. It was his way to try and cut my support and succeed in controlling me, as he did later on with my family members too. This is just one of many, many episodes over the nine years I was married.

One fine day, I got a letter saying I had a court hearing related to some driving issues. I called to ask what happened and they informed me that I had accumulated 12 points on my licence and that I was going to be banned from driving for six months. I was in utter shock and disbelief. I immediately called his mother to tell her what happened, and she just kept saying how wrong this was. Yet, a few weeks later, we were in the house all together when I saw him sign some papers and he had told me "I am giving you some points". I did not question it in fear of the abuse and aggressive behaviour. In effect, I was afraid of him. So, to keep the peace I did not say anything.

For the first time in my life, I was summoned to court. The whole experience was surreal. I was told by a judge that I could not drive for six months. I left that courtroom feeling dirty, as though I had just been the most dishonest person in the world. I had just taken a hit for him and the worst bit is he did not care. He just laughed it off saying "ah it's ok, you'll get around in taxis".

There are a few moments in life where you never forget how you felt. That was one of them. I thought to myself "who am I?" I was not true to myself and it just felt so bad inside. But then there were times where he would say the most caring things like "oh what would I do without you, I love you so much, I can't imagine life without you". I learned now that at the time this was his convenience. I was filling a space. He needed someone to look after him, to cook, to bring children up, but there was no depth to it – at least this is how I feel about it.

We had a second and then a third child and at that point, we decided to move countries. All along, he had been blaming his mood swings and behaviour on his stressful position at work. One day we sat down and wrote a list of Pros and Cons for each country and decided to move away for a better quality of life. We always knew the money would be less, but we would have a better work-life balance. We loaded two trucks, furniture and all, bought new things for our house, and waved the van goodbye together. The kids and I moved, but he never did. What I realise now is that he never had any intention of making the move. For him, it was just another adventure or thrill which he thrived on. Living in a hot country, sunbathing, the beach.

We lived apart for a while, but we both knew this was unsustainable, so I kept asking him for a date for his permanent move, and it was never a good time. Either because the economy is not doing well so we cannot sell the businesses now, or because the Sterling is not doing well, or any other excuse you can imagine. I began to get the feeling that this move would never actually happen. Some of my friends used to say that if he wants to be with his family he would not care about this money and would just come, but I would try and excuse him by regurgitating all that he told me.

I found myself finding excuses for his behaviour many times, especially with my family. There was one episode where I clearly remember him calling my Dad from abroad, to not allow me to go to a family party where everyone was going. When my Dad started talking to me about it, I told him "he doesn't OWN me. You are all going to this party and I am coming too!". I mean, when I look back now, I cringe at the thought of being so controlled. How could I, an educated woman, a professional, a mother, let myself get into this relationship which was clearly so toxic. At the time, I felt I did not have a way out.

He was becoming more arrogant, had a sense of entitlement beyond belief, and was outright horrible with me. I felt like I had lost myself in this process called *marriage*. Surely it was not supposed to feel like this.? But I was brought up thinking marriage is for life and there is good in everyone, so I stayed. Hoping for change, hoping for a better life, hoping that one day he would suddenly realise how his behaviour affected the whole family. But that day never came.

I hadn't read anything about narcissism until his sister, who knew him well, sent me a book about it. When I read it, it was like reading my life story. He fell into the category like a glove. Terms like *gaslighting* and *flying monkeys* came to life and I could see how his behaviour had been enabled all his life (possibly even unknowingly) by family and people close to him.

One morning, I woke up and it all just hit me. I was changing into a person who was a million miles away from who I was inside. I was lying in bed thinking does it even matter if I get out of bed or not? Does it even matter if I am alive or not? I am useless. And that is when I realised that this life I was living was not normal. I realised that this was unacceptable for me, but most of all for my kids.

Yes, marriage has its ups and downs. Yes, you get married for the good and the bad, but this was far more than that. This man had taken away everything from me. I had nothing. I had no sense of self. I had not many people to talk to about it. I mean, where would I start? I just realised then that if a change did not happen, this was like a boiling pot and something was about to burst. I spoke to his Mum who knew everything, every argument, every bit of abuse that was going on, and even she told me "you have to leave for a better life".

Abuse comes in many shapes and forms. It is not always the bruises on your face or body. The silent treatment is abuse, demanding sex is abuse, humiliating you is abuse, being told you are stupid is abuse, mocking you in private or public is abuse, and when these things happen regularly it is no wonder you lose all confidence and feel so helpless. This is NOT love.

To date, he is engaging less and less with our three children as well as not meeting his maintenance obligations despite being well off. I live with worries that they could suffer too. I try my best to supplement his role in bringing them all up to be happy, driven by strong values and education. But above all, I want them to have the self-respect and confidence to stand up to things that are not right.

My advice for women in narcissistic relationships is this - follow your gut. We hear this expression all the time and we overlook it, but it is the truth. Your mind KNOWS you are in the wrong place and that these things should not be happening. But for whatever reason - be it low self-esteem, low confidence, fear of failure, love - you settle for a mediocre, unhappy coupled life.

I have only one regret- I waited nine years living in hope and did not leave sooner. I have three wonderful children, but the rest for him seems like it never happened and he does not have a care for, yet it has scarred me for life. I have started loving myself and finding ways to do that, but it has been very hard. I have had such a painful journey, but I do believe that in pain there is growth, and I will not let the wounds define who I am. They have made me stronger and more determined to go and chase MY dreams, on MY terms.

I still have a long road ahead but I am sure that if I can inspire women to be true to themselves, and really know their worth, then fewer people will have the traumatic experiences that I had.

MEET THE AUTHOR

Donna Anne Pace is a proud mother of six children and a Successful Women in Business Award Winner 'Overcoming Adversity' 2019. In March 2018, Donna self-published her first book, The Reinvention of Me - a journey of self-discovery in a disenchanted world in 2018, of which has been featured in local and international media around the world.

Donna decided to write her very first book after her daily life went on a downward spiral in 2014. Life became very alien to Donna as she adjusted to a new home, living alone without her beloved children, facing financial difficulty, family estrangement, and filing for divorce. Donna needed to find sense and meaning in her life, and in 2017, she started journaling her thoughts, feelings and past experiences every day. One year later, and in her new one bedroom flat, Donna accomplished writing and self-publishing her first book; created a website; passed the ECDL Level 2 Certificate; set up her small business OneVoiceMyChoice.co.uk, and achieved one of her lifetime goals – became an Author!

Donna's public speaking engagements in the UK and Malta;

November 2018 – 'It Shouldn't Hurt To Be' Conference on Domestic Violence, on behalf of the Labour Party for Women (Nisa Laburisti)

May 2019 - YouTrust and Dragonfly Project, Dorset
Conference on Domestic Violence

June 2019 – Interview with BBC Spotlight

October 2019 – BBC Radio Solent and Wessex FM
with regards to Donna's local initiative of a new
school uniform bank for parents on low incomes
and/or facing a toxic environment.

November 2019 - 'The Power of Positive' Conference on behalf of the Maltese Government, Foundation for Social Welfare Services (FSWS).

November 2019 – University of Malta, Studenti Harsein Socjali (SHS) Event, 'Stop the Silence'.

November 2019 – Guest on Illum ma' Steph with thanks to TV Presenter, Stephanie Spiteri.

May 2020 – ONE Radio Malta, interview with Radio Presenter and President of Nisa Laburisiti, Nikita Zammit Alamango.

Donna Anne Pace is a member of the Successful Women in Business in the South West of England; the Women's Equality Party S.W. and is also a Global Sister of the Global Sisterhood 501(c)(3) USA.

This mission for Donna's small business is to help empower, support, educate, and inspire women to find their voice and learn how to reinvent their lives!

"Changing The Narrative To Change Lives"

Acknowledgments

- National Centre for Biotechnology Information
- biblegateway.com
- cps.gov.uk
- psychologytoday.com
- wellandgood.com
- womensaid.org.uk
- rightsofwomen.org.uk
- ncdsv.org (DC Coaltion Against DV)
- Successful Women in Business SWIB
- refuge.org.uk
- J.K. Rowling, Author of Harry Potter Books & Films
- divorce-online.co.uk
- nhs.uk
- gov.uk
- acesdv.org
- dshs.wa.gov
- psychecentral.com
- savelives.org.uk
- hse.gov.uk
- Nisa Laburisti
- YouTrust
- Dragonfly Project
- BBC Spotlight
- BBC Radio Solent
- Wessex FM
- Government of Malta

- FSWS
- University of Malta
- Studenti Harsien Socjali
- Stephanie Spiteri, Illum ma' Steph
- Nikita Zammit Alamango, President of Nisa Laburisti and Radio Presenter
- ONE Radio Malta
- The Office for National Statistics

GLOSSARY

Abuse - We define domestic abuse as an incident or pattern of incidents of controlling, coercive, threatening, degrading and violent behaviour, including sexual violence, in the majority of cases by a partner or ex-partner, but also by a family member or carer. It is very common. In the vast majority of cases it is experienced by women and is perpetrated by men. (womensaid.org.uk)

Abuser - a person who uses abusive tactics and behaviors to exert power and control over another person with whom the abuser is in an intimate, dating, or family relationship. (ncdsv.org)

Advocate - a trained professional or volunteer working for a non-profit or government-based domestic violence or victim-witness advocate program. (ncdsv.org)

Attorney: a person legally appointed or hired by a respondent or petitioner to represent her/him in legal matters. (ncdsv.org)

Compassion Fatigue: a state of exhaustion where one feels depleted, helpless, and hopeless about work, life, and the state of the world. (ncdsv.org)

Contempt: violation of one or more terms of a protection order (TPO/CPO) by the respondent, USA.(ncdsv.org)

Controlling or coercive behaviour - Controlling behaviour is a range of acts designed to make a person subordinate and/or dependant by isolating them from sources of support, exploiting their resources and capacities for personal gain, depriving them of the means needed for independence, resistance and escape, and regulating their everyday behaviour. (CPS.gov.uk)

Coercive behaviour is an act or a pattern of acts of assaults, threats, humiliation, and intimidation or other abuse that is used to harm, punish, or frighten their victim. (CPS.gov.uk)

Criminal Contempt: The judge finds the respondent violated a provision of the TPO/CPO that is criminal in nature. Examples include but are not limited to; failing to stay away from the petitioner or another protected party named in the TPO/CPO, contacting the petitioner or another protected party, committing assault, sexual assault, malicious destruction of property, or harassment. (ncdsv.org)

Dating Violence: domestic violence that occurs between people who are dating. This is the preferred term to use when describing abusive teenage relationships. (ncdsv.org)

Divorce Petition - A divorce petition, otherwise known as D8 form, marks the start of your divorce process. A divorce petition is a form that is filled out by one spouse (the petitioner) and is filed and sent to the other (the respondent). (divorce-online.co.uk)

Domestic Violence - Domestic abuse, or domestic violence, is defined across Government as any incident of controlling, coercive or threatening behaviour, violence, or abuse between those aged 16 or over who are or have been intimate partners or family members, regardless of their gender or sexuality. (CPS.gov.uk)

Economic/Financial Abuse - when a batterer uses finances to establish and maintain power and control over a victim. Examples include, but are not limited to, controlling a partner's finances, taking the victim's money without permission, giving the victim an allowance, prohibiting/limiting a victim's access to bank accounts or credit cards, denying the victim the right to work, and/or sabotaging a victim's credit. (ncdsv.org)

Emergency/Temporary Shelter: immediate, confidential, and safe housing for victims of domestic violence who are fleeing abuse; can be through a domestic violence program or at an undisclosed hotel. (ncdsv.org)

Emotional/psychological abuse - when a batterer uses emotions, self-esteem, and/or a person's mental state to establish and maintain power and control over a victim. Examples include, but are not limited to, putting the victim down or making the victim feel bad about her/himself, calling the victim names, playing mind games, making the victim think s/he is crazy, making the victim feel guilty, and/or humiliating the victim. (ncdsv.org)

Female Genital Mutilation (FGM) - Female Genital Mutilation (FGM) is a collective term for a range of procedures that involve partial or total removal of the external female genitalia for non-medical reasons. It is sometimes referred to as female circumcision or female genital cutting. The practice is medically unnecessary, is extremely painful, and has serious health consequences, both at the time when the mutilation is carried out, and in later life. (CPS.gov.uk)

Fibromyalgia - Fibromyalgia, also called fibromyalgia syndrome (FMS), is a long-term condition that causes pain all over the body. (nhs.uk)

Forced Marriage - A forced marriage is where one or both people do not (or in cases of people with learning disabilities or reduced capacity, cannot) consent to the marriage as they are pressurised, or abuse is used, to force them to do so. It is recognised in the UK as a form of domestic or child abuse and a serious abuse of human rights. (gov.uk)

Gaslighting - a tactic in which a person or entity, to gain more power, makes a victim question their reality. It works much better than you may think. Anyone is susceptible to gaslighting, and it is a common technique of abusers, dictators, narcissists, and cult leaders. It is done slowly, so the victim doesn't realize how much they've been brainwashed. For example, in the movie Gaslight (1944), a man manipulates his wife to the point where she thinks she is losing her mind. (psychologytoday.com)

Hate Crime - can be used to describe a range of criminal behaviour where the perpetrator is motivated by hostility or demonstrates hostility towards the victim's disability, race, religion, sexual orientation, or transgender identity. (cps.gov.uk)

Honor-based violence & forced marriage - So-called 'honour- based' violence is a crime or incident committed to protect or defend the so-called honour of the family or community. The term can cover a collection of practices used to control behaviour within families or other social groups, to protect perceived cultural and religious beliefs or honour. These crimes are included within the domestic abuse definition, but may also be carried out by people who are not partners or family members. (CPS.gov.uk)

IDVA – Independent Domestic Violence Advisers

Intimidation - when one person uses threats to cause another person fear and/or to coerce her/him into doing something. Examples include, but are not limited to: making someone afraid by using looks, actions, gestures, and/or a loud voice, destroying property, abusing pets, and/or displaying weapons. (ncdsv.org)

Isolation - Isolation is a form of abuse often closely connected to controlling behaviors. It is not an isolated behavior, but the outcome of many kinds of abusive behaviors. By keeping the victim from seeing who they want to see, doing what they want to do, setting and meeting goals, and controlling how the victim thinks and feels, the perpetrator is isolating the victim from the resources (personal and public) which may help them leave the relationship. (acesdv.org)

Love bombing - A love bomb refers to the form of emotional manipulation in which a person, often a narcissist, "bombs" you with an OTT amount of affection, flattery, gifts, and praise early in the

185

relationship in order to win over your attention for the purpose of being able to control you. (wellandgood.com)

MARAC – Multi Agency Risk Assessment Conference

Mental mistreatment or emotional abuse is deliberately causing mental or emotional pain. Examples include intimidation, coercion, ridiculing, harassment, treating an adult like a child, isolating an adult from family, friends, or regular activity, use of silence to control behavior, and yelling or swearing which results in mental distress. (dshs.wa.gov)

Narcissist - The symptoms of narcissistic personality disorder include: grandiose sense of importance, preoccupation with unlimited success, belief that one is special and unique, exploitative of others, lack of empathy, arrogance, and jealousy of others. These symptoms cause significant distress in a person's life. (psychcentral.com)

Non-Molestation Order - A non-molestation order is aimed at preventing your partner or ex-partner from using or threatening violence against you or your child, or intimidating, harassing or pestering you, to ensure the health, safety, and well-being of yourself and your children. (womensaid.org.uk)

Occupation Order - An occupation order regulates who can live in the family home, and can also restrict your abuser from entering the surrounding area. If you do not feel safe continuing to live with your partner, or if you have left home because of violence, but want to return and exclude your abuser, you may want to apply for an occupation order. (cps.gov.uk)

Online platforms are increasingly used to perpetrate domestic abuse. Online domestic abuse can include behaviours such as monitoring of social media profiles or emails, abuse over social media such as Facebook or Twitter, sharing intimate photos or videos without your consent, using GPs locators or spyware. (womensaid.org.uk)

Perpetrator - a person carrying out domestic violence behaviors. (ncdsv.org)

Petitioner - In the Family Court, the party who started the proceedings by making an application is usually called the Petitioner. (cps.gov.uk)

Physical abuse - when a perpetrator uses his/her body or other objects to cause harm or injury to establish and maintain power and control over a victim. Examples include, but are not limited to: hitting, kicking, biting, pushing, scratching, slapping, strangling, beating, using a weapon against another person, punching, throwing, burning, poisoning, stabbing, and shooting. (ncdsv.org)

Power & Control Wheel - a tool many advocates use to illustrate abusive tactics and behaviors used by batterers against victims.

Pre-dominant Aggressor - the person who poses the most serious ongoing threat in a domestic violence situation. (ncdsv.org)

Protection Order - the general term for an order issued by the Court mandating a batterer to not contact, harass, or come within a certain distance of the petitioner and/or other persons named in the order. (ncdsv.org)

Psychological abuse - Psychological abuse involves the regular and deliberate use of a range of words and non-physical actions used with the purpose to manipulate, hurt, weaken or frighten a person mentally and emotionally; and/or distort, confuse or influence a person's thoughts and actions within their everyday lives, changing their sense of self and harming their wellbeing. (safelives.org.uk)

PTSD - a psychological disorder that can occur in an individual after s/he has suffered a traumatic event (such as domestic violence) and is characterized by flashbacks, avoidance of things that may trigger a memory of the traumatic event, and a significantly heightened state of alert. (ncdsv.org)

Respondent - The party responding to the application is called the respondent. There can be more than one respondent. (cps.gov.uk)

Restraining Order - If the police charge your abuser and the case goes to the criminal courts then the court may make a restraining order to protect you. The criminal court can make the restraining order whether or not your abuser is convicted. (rightsofwomen.org.uk)

Revenge porn - sharing private sexual materials with intent to cause distress (gov.uk)

Safety Plan - a plan, verbal or written, that a victim of domestic violence creates with an advocate. The plan consists of action steps a victim can take to keep her/his children safe when violence takes place or to stop violence from happening. (ncdsv.org)

Secondary Trauma - a risk we incur when we engage compassionately or empathetically with a traumatized adult or child. (ncdsv.org)

Sexual Abuse - when a perpetrator uses sexual acts to establish and maintain power and control over a victim without her/his consent. Examples include, but are not limited to: making the victim do sexual things against her/his will, sexual assault, treating the victim like a sex object, forcing sex after violence, and/or forcing the victim to watch pornography. (ncdsv.org)

Sexual Assault - any unwanted sexual activity forced on one person by another. (ncdsv.org)

Stalking and harassment occur not only in a domestic abuse setting – people can be stalked by strangers or acquaintances too. (CPS.gov.uk)

Stalking is a specific type of harassment, often described as a pattern of unwanted, fixated, or obsessive behaviour which is intrusive and causes fear of violence or serious alarm and distress. For example, a person following, watching, or spying on someone else, or forcing contact with them through social media, might be considered as stalking. (CPS.gov.uk)

Harassment offences involve a 'course of conduct,' or repeated actions, which could be expected to cause distress or fear in any reasonable person. This will often include repeated attempts to impose unwanted contact or communication on someone. (CPS.gov.uk)

Survivor - a person who was or is being abused or harmed by another person. (ncdsv.org)

Trauma - experiencing an event that causes injury or stress to a person's physical or psychological well-being. (ncdsv.org)

Victim - a person who is abused, harmed, or killed by another person. (ncdsv.org)

Witness Statement - is a document recording the evidence of a person, which is signed by that person to confirm that the contents of the statement are true (hse.gov.uk)

DOMESTIC VIOLENCE CHARITIES & ORGANISATIONS (UK)

http://www.elderabuse.org.uk/

http://www.bawso.org.uk/

http://www.brokenrainbow.org.uk/home

http://www.signhealth.org.uk/deafhope/

http://www.eavesforwomen.org.uk/

http://www.getconnected.org.uk/

http://www.help@galop.org.uk

http://imkaan.org.uk/

http://www.stalkinghelpline.org/

http://www.rapecrisis.org.uk/

http://www.refuge.org.uk/

http://www.rightsofwomen.org.uk/

http://england.shelter.org.uk/

https://www.victimsupport.org.uk/

http://www.womensaid.org.uk/http://www.england.shelter.org.uk/

http://www.rightsofwomen.org.uk/get-advice/family-la

https://www.gov.uk/report-domestic-abuse

https://www.familylives.org.uk/

https://www.judiciary.uk/announcements/coro
navirus-crisis-guidance-on-compliance-with-
family-court-child-arrangement-orders/

http://www.turn2us.org.uk/

https://survivingeconomicabuse.org/

http://www.signhealth.org.uk/

USA DV CHARITIES & ORGANISATIONS

https://www.thehotline.org/

https://www.milagrosday.org/

https://www.safehorizon.org/

http://www.ncadv.org

http://www.evawintl.org

http://www.feedmhc.org

http://www.futureswithoutviolence.org

http://www.globalfundforwomen.org

http://www.homeaid.org

http://www.ivatcenters.org

http://www.iwdc.org

http://www.nlada.org

http://forwomen.org

http://nnedv.org/

http://www.nowfoundation.org/

http://www.nwlc.org/

http://www.voicesandfaces.org/

http://www.save.org/

http://wccww.wordpress.com/

https://www.globalsisterhoodonline.org/

https://www.rbrw.org/

The National Domestic Violence Hotline: It's available around the clock and in more than 200 Languages: call 1-800-799-SAFE or text LOVEIS to 22522

Anti-Violence Project: offers a 24-hour English/Spanish hotline for LGBTQ+ people experiencing abuse or hate-based violence: call 212-714-1141

New York State Domestic and Sexual Violence Hotline: is available in multiple languages: call 1-800-9426906 for English. For deaf or hard of hearing dial 711

MALTESE HELPLINE NUMBERS

(Commission on Domestic Violence @cdvmalta)

Kellimni	kellimni.com
SupportLine	179
Police Emergency Line	112
Appogg	22959000
Legal Aid	25674330
Victim Support Malta	21228333
Social Work Unit Gozo	21556630
Mental Health Malta	23304313
Dar Merhba Bik	21440035
Dar Emmaus	21552390
SOAR Support Group (SJAF)	21808981
Women's Rights Foundation	800 621 49
Free Legal Helpline	
Rainbow Support Service (LGBTIQ)	21430009
Fondazzjoni Dar il-Hena	27888211
Programm Sebh-Dar Qalb ta'Gesu	21482504

WHO ARE WE?

We are Survivors, not Victims

WHY ARE WE?

Because we are brave and we are strong

WHAT ARE WE?

We are Global Warriors!

BACKLIST

The Reinvention of Me – a journey of self-discovery in
a disenchanted world.

Printed in Poland
by Amazon Fulfillment
Poland Sp. z o.o., Wrocław

58804369R00117